I'LL BE BACK

Harold Freedlander • 1913–2002

This project is dedicated to Harold,
in loving memory, from his family.

I'LL BE BACK

Harold Freedlander's World War II Letters
to the Home Front

EDITED AND COMPILED BY
Lois Freedlander
Ann Freedlander Hunt
Mimi Freedlander McCain

The Wooster Book Company
WOOSTER • OHIO
2002

The Wooster Book Company
205 West Liberty Street
Wooster Ohio • 44691
www.woosterbook.com

ISBN 1-888683-98-8

An Appreciation

We all know him. We have all benefitted from his generosity. And, we have all learned from him.

Harold Freedlander needs little introduction in the city of Wooster, Ohio. Here is the store owner who will open an account based on knowing the newcomer's next door neighbor. And, on personal appeal, will open the store during off-hours for a special (read "neglectful") customer. Here is the store owner who helps a customer try on a coat and then offers an honest assessment. Here is the store owner who thinks of his employees in the same way a teacher thinks of his students.

There was more than just retailing going on here. This was the conscientious and committed establishment of a way to conduct business that became the standard for an entire community.

This alone is a remarkable accomplishment and a considerable legacy. But also in this community, we enjoy an extensive public park, a swimming pool, and a wonderful proscenium theater, all with the same Freedlander name.

Perhaps the easiest thing to do after a long career in a business that swelled to hundreds of employees and became one of the largest independent department stores in the midwest would be to enjoy the satisfactions of a job well done. But, this brief introduction affords me a place to say thank you once again to a gentleman who took time as a retired executive to counsel and coach many would-be entrepreneurs, including myself.

And so, we have established our own business very much within the shadow of Harold Freedlander's business. Not only carrying into it much of his well-offered advice, but also attempting to maintain the basic principles upon which his business values, and indeed our community values, are based.

One day, Mrs Freedlander mentioned Harold's letters to me—letters written during the first years of their marriage while Harold served in the Second World War. What a surprise to see Lois, with great dignity and poise, carrying a mound of boxes containing all his thoughts and a full catalogue of his experiences. There were 379 letters in all and every one full of charm and wit and insight.

Harold had completed his undergraduate education at Harvard in Modern European History, and now he was in the middle of history being made. He is not only an informed and acute observer of the world situation he was thrust into, but committed to fundamental principles of democracy and self determination.

But these letters are not the dry stuff of solid men fighting in a global conflict of unquestioned necessity. In all ways and in all senses, these are love letters—a wonderful outpouring to Lois of love and romance and devotion and optimism and encouragement for a life that will be celebrated for a very long time together.

The project of collecting and assembling these letters into a coherent collection was a fascinating undertaking. More importantly, it served as a reminder of the legacy that this man among us had earned and a reminder of even more that he has to share. And in the final analysis, these letters also remind us that the strength of the heart—that true love—is all sustaining.

To the magnificent Freedlander family this project became a tribute to their beloved Harold, and for Harold's daughters, this project became an introduction to a new aspect of their father—and to the establishment of their family's principles—that, I hope, is a life-long benefit.

Recently Ann Freedlander Hunt wrote, "I have learned so much about my dad during his WWII experiences. Editing this book meant so much to me. It was a labor of love as well as a personal history lesson." And Mimi told me, "As I read each letter, I could visualize my dad as I came to know him—always loving, always caring, always motivating."

I think many others will find much to learn and enjoy from these letters and it is from us, the readers, neighbors, customers, and community members that this book is dedicated with love and respect to the Freedlander family.

—DAVID WIESENBERG
The Wooster Book Company

I'LL BE BACK

January 3, 1943

Dear Folks,

The Army is fine since I spoke to you an hour ago. Today we had shots, exams, and insurance signing. I am sending you some documents, Lo, that you should keep.

We were up at 5:00. The food is good, but it's quite a novelty to eat it all from one tray.

Within a few days we'll get orders and then will come the real beginning. It's quite an experience already.

I hope I get the work I asked for, but you can never tell.

I sent my civies home today. I hope you all feel well and shall really get down to writing in a few days. I must shave now (electric—think of that!).

You all know how much I love you and think of you and also how proud I am to be doing my duty.

All my love, Harold

〰

January 8, 1943

Dear Lois, Mom & Dad,

We've had our first two drills and like all the rest of the rookies, I have two left feet.

We're in a fine platoon with a very nice sergeant and a good corporal. There are still almost a dozen of us Wooster boys together for basic training which begins today and lasts either 8 or 13 weeks. None of us has been assigned yet, but this camp has anti-aircraft, coast artillery, signal corps, and adjutant-general branches. Yesterday we took another aptitude test. I haven't the slightest idea where I'll end up—except for being away from all of you, it's a good life.

During this basic training period we have no weekend passes. Galveston is an old wharf town and not very attractive, and Houston is too far (40 miles) for an evening's jaunt. There is a guest house here.

My visiting time is very limited. After basic training, furloughs and even permanent arrangements are possible depending on where I land.

This is a good camp. We are very well fed and have good officers.

The trip down was secret—we didn't know where we were going until we got here. We passed thru Dayton, St. Louis, Little Rock, Texarkana, and Houston.

Well, chow call is coming up. Perhaps I'll be able to call next Saturday night but don't be disappointed if I don't. They really put it to us and I may not be able to leave the battery area if I have work to do.

I'm waiting for your first letter and want the news.

Each of you kiss each other for me. Lois, dearest, keep your chin up—this isn't forever, nor I hope, very long.

All my love to all of you.

Ever yours, Harold

P.S. Just took out an hour to mop barracks. Saturday is inspection.

Boy, Snooks, will I make you a good wife when I come home.

⌒

January 8, 1943

Dear Snooky,

First of all I want you to know how much I love you—and that for me this is just the way any man should take to protect the dearest person in the world—you.

I've shown your photograph to the boys (out of 39 men in this barracks, 25 are married) and you're the prettiest Army wife in the 2nd platoon.

There are some fine men here. Army life is at its best in the companionship it affords the men. We're very lucky so many of us from Wooster are together.

The Army consists of following orders and doing your best. In addition, I love the drill and am learning to execute commands and salute in a "military" manner. I love that kind of stuff.

This is a beautiful camp. I have to admit that we are not roughing it much; everything's modern. I feel fine and I suppose life in the open makes me ready for bed at 9 o'clock.

I hope you're feeling OK. This separation, however hard for us both, is temporary and necessary. We are together in spirit. You know how I love you—and in our case absence makes the flame even brighter.

I love you now and forever and most passionately my darling. I live, as you do, for the day we are again together. Meanwhile, carry on, as I shall.

Ever your adoring, Harold

⌐⌐

January 9, 1943

Dear Folks,

After three hectic and confusing days in Columbus, we are in Texas. Twelve of us from Wooster are still together.

This camp is a Coast Artillery Camp which surprised Kenny Fowler and me particularly since we'd both made highest grades in classification tests and asked for quartermaster corps. But the Army hears you out and then sends you where they need men. I am encouraged that they asked whether I would consider officers training. It will be hard but I'll take a crack at it.

There are about 13,000 men here. We are in a well-equipped barracks. The dining hall has flowers, drapes, and paper napkins. This place is located 15 miles inland from Galveston and 45 miles from Houston. When I know more I'll advise you when to come down for your winter vacation.

Right now the loud speaker is playing music by Tommy Dorsey and Charlie Barnett.

Of course, I miss all of you more than I can say, but this is a necessary thing and, after all, I'm just doing my part to protect our future.

The trip down was all new to me. I couldn't let you know when and where I was going and that's why I didn't call you before I left Fort Hayes.

I hope everything is well at home. Keep going and keep busy. And write often. Every man in service waits at mail call with his tongue hanging out. Air-mail is 2 days, regular about 5 days.

I love you very much and shall wait to hear from you—and soon to see you.

Ever and always your, Harold

∽

Sunday, 8:30 A.M.
January 10, 1943

Dearest Lois, Mom and Dad,

After we left Wooster last Saturday (it seems like a lot longer, doesn't it?), we proceeded to Fort Hayes. We got in about 6:30 and immediately had inspection and supper. They issued blankets and we were in bed at 9:00.

Sunday was a full day. We were up at 5:10 A.M. After chow (chow is Army for all meals) we took our classification test. Out of 150 questions, I answered 133, and got a 1 rating with a grade of 140. Kenny Fowler, a buddy of mine, who has taught school in Wooster for some years only got 139, so I feel pretty good. Following that exam, we took two more—a mechanical aptitude test and a radio test. Fort Hayes is a very peculiar place. It is very old and continually crowded with new men coming in. The food there is poor—here, wonderful.

After noon chow we went back to the drill hall and were issued uniforms. They have you strip down to your identification tags, give you two barracks bags, and start you down a long counter. In 1/2 hour you are thru—you have 2 OD shirts and pants, 1 OD blouse (jacket), 1 OD garrison cap, 2 suntan shirts and pants and caps, 2 suits of 2-piece long undies, 3 shirts and shorts, 4 handkerchiefs, 1 raincoat, 2 pair G.I. shoes, 1 overcoat, a zipper-front windbreaker, 2 towels and toilet kit,

2 fatigue shirts and pants, and 1 fatigue hat. These last are work clothes and we all look like "Peter Plink" in them and wear them a good part of every day. Following issuing of equipment, we got a typhoid shot and a vaccination. By the time we got thru, we picked up our barracks bags with all this stuff in including our civvies. It weighed 70 pounds. We carried them clear across camp to our barracks. I kept my brown shoes as I can wear them off duty. Sunday evening Wayne Frary and I went downtown for dinner and I had the thrill of talking to you—so far the high spot of this adventure. I shall do my best to call on Saturday, January 23rd, as that will be the best way I can think of to spend our anniversary, darling.

Monday, we were assigned to drill hall detail. For me it was very amusing to be behind the counter passing out clothes to guys who thought I was a veteran. It was only the day before that I had been in their place and it was kind of fun to say, "Come on now, you're not dead are you? Put it in the bag!"

Monday evening we played bridge in barracks until lights out. Lights are out at 9:00 but you can use the service clubs until 11:00. Tuesday at 5:30 they awoke us and Fowler, O'Dell, Johnson, Brenneman, Vizzo, Stewart, Horst, Rower, and I from Wooster, and Johnny Grande and Sam Davidson were ordered to report to the orderly room. We were told to turn in our bedding and pack our barracks bags and be back in 15 minutes. That meant only one thing. Back to barracks we tore, said goodbye to Claude Hendershot, Billy Hail, Bill Frye, Al Coppola, and all the rest of the gang. At 8 o'clock they had us fed and by 9:00 we were in the pullmans. The train didn't leave until 11:00 but due to the necessity for protecting troop trains, they get you out as fast as possible to prevent any leak and possible sabotage.

At 11 o'clock Tuesday A.M. we pulled out of Columbus. We traveled exactly 48 hours arriving at Camp Wallace. The group was in charge of a 2nd Lieutenant and a Sergeant and they did everything possible to make us comfortable. We ate all our meals in the dining car except supper Tuesday evening in St. Louis and breakfast Thursday morning in Houston. All day Wednesday, passing thru Arkansas (which is the most God-awful hole I have ever seen), we played bridge—quite a tournament. I think the Lieutenant would have liked to join us, but of course he couldn't.

Fort Wallace is not in a town. The train stopped at a place about the size of Creston called Hitchcock. There the Army trucks met us and brought us here. The first day we were assigned to barracks and issued bedding.

Now, what is Camp Wallace? It is a pretty good-sized place, about 15,000 men here. The principal job here is anti-aircraft and coast artillery—40 mm and 90 mm coast guns. This is only a basic training camp. For some reason I have been assigned to artillery.

This is not front line work in any sense. Many batteries are permanently assigned to ack-ack (anti-aircraft) duty in cities, and all of the stuff we have fired from well behind our own lines. This is not infantry but you can see a good deal of action. In a couple of weeks I'll know more, and I may be given supply work.

Artillery is composed as follows: There are four platoons of about 75 men each to a battery, in infantry a company having approximately 300 men at full strength. There are four such batteries, or 1200 men to a battalion (in infantry that would be a brigade). Two or three battalions are attached to a regiment of infantry in battle or are used detached as occasions demand.

In cities like New York, batteries of anti-aircraft and coast artillery operate independently of battalion strength. I hope that gives you a rough idea of this kind of outfit. I am in Btry (Battery) B 32nd CATB (32nd Coast Artillery Training Battalion). We are the 2nd platoon and will be principally concerned with anti-aircraft in a few weeks when we get to play with the pretty little 30 mm anti-aircrafts which shoot accurately up to one mile up.

Friday they took all us rookies to the drill field and taught us left face, right face, about face, right dress, attention, parade rest, at ease, and the salute. We also did a little column marching.

Yesterday we had our first dress inspection of barracks. (Saturday is traditionally inspection day in the Army.) The Captain gave us a commendation and said he was proud of the job after one week in the service. Boy—do I make a neat bed—hospital corners and everything.

In the afternoon we went to the Camp Wallace "county fair" which is held in the drill grounds. It is a quicky of what a soldier gets in his basic training.

We will have obstacle race running, calisthenics, hikes with rifle and full pack, rifle drill, care and shooting of a 30.06 calibre Army Springfield rifle, ju jitsu, wrestling and judo (nerve pressure wrestling), military courtesy, inspections, drill, and finally, near the end of our 13 weeks, training on the ack-acks and maneuvers. Of course there is radio and searchlight work too. We were issued rifles yesterday.

The finest thing about the Army is the close companionship you get with the men. The only tough thing is our separation. After the first couple of weeks here, I will let you know when the best time to come might be.

> I'm waiting for that mail.
> Love and kisses,
> Ever,
> Your, Harold

P.S. Write all the news and plan to spend part of February near here so we can be together part of the time. You can spend 8 days in camp at the guest house.

⌒

My Darling,

The radio is playing "I'll Kiss Your Picture Goodnight." Well, that's just how I feel. If your connections were right you should be pulling into Cleveland now. I hope you had a pleasant and comfortable trip. I can see you stepping into the terminal, and see the expression on your Mother and Dad's face as they greet you. It makes me feel better to know how happy they will be.

Tomorrow I go on the line. You know what that means. Secret! I'm going to start to study my IDR (Infantry Drill Regulations) again. I hope I'll do a good job—I think I can. It will take me a few weeks to catch on, but the strictly military part of this has always appealed to me. One fly in the ointment is that I have to stand retreat at 5:45 during the summer. I think I can make that 6:05 bus. If I can't, I'll need a car or get a permanent ride. After September, retreat will move back to 5:30 which will be a snap. NOTE: Address my letters (by rank) according to the return address. Don't jump the gun—it isn't considered funny here.

My love to Mother and Dad and Mother and Dad—and a great big hug and a kiss for my baby. I love you, and can hardly wait until I see you.

Ever yours, and with oceans of love,

Harold

              ↫

July 11, 1943
Camp Wallace, Texas

Hello Darling,

Here I am on Weekend CQ—the very first weekend after you've gone. I've got a good book, the radio, and the Sicilian invasion to think about—plus you. I hope you'll excuse the typewriter but I'm here in the office. (I even sleep here tonight and tomorrow night.)

How is it to be back in Cleveland? It is surely strange for me to be spending a Saturday night in camp—my first in six months.

The radio is playing "Oh, How I Miss You Tonight"—and I do. The week has gone fast—with my new duties.

I'll bet you and Mother are still talking away. Do you already feel far away from this corner of Texas, or are you itching to come back? I hope the latter—because I now know what I guessed all along—that the Army agreed with me because you were here.

My private barber gave me a pretty good haircut last night—but not a G.I. I hope not to have one of those for a long time. I've got a rifle to worry about again, along with a cartridge belt and bayonet. I'm kind of anxious to get out on the range and try out the new model Garand. I'm going to try to get the 1st Sergeant to send me out next week. He bought me a sandwich and bottle of beer to cheer my vigil tonight and since then, twenty people, including a lieutenant and two staff sergeants, have been in to shoot the bull. So I haven't gotten much reading done. No one will be here tomorrow, so I'm sure I'll get started on *Northwest Passage*. I must have everything brought to me because I cannot leave the Battery area. I am responsible for the work here tonight.

The news from Sicily seems good and we hope it keeps up. This is the real thing. We won't stop with just Sicily—I think the High Command will point thru Italy to the heart of the Axis—the German heartland. We will have reverses but we are winning the campaign already.

I'm thinking of you every minute of the day, sweetheart, and looking forward just three weeks when I will be heading north and east. Give my love to the folks.

All my love and kisses, darling and write often.

Every and always yours, Harold

〰

Dearest,

It's 2:30 Sunday afternoon and I'm all alone in the office. The *Army Hour* is being broadcast over the PA system and I've taken time off. From now until tomorrow morning most everyone will be out. I expect to get a major portion of *Northwest Passage* read.

You have probably wondered how I am doing on the line. I am giving some first aid instruction, and assisting in bayonet and grenade training for basics. I find the hardest thing to get used to is drilling men in simple infantry drill. I haven't had too much of that previously, only a few weeks in OCS, and have to be on my toes all the time to keep from marching men in a ditch, or something worse—into other men.

This has been a rainy day. A perfect day to curl up with a good book! In fact, it's very restful to stay in camp over the weekend. I shall surely spend one more weekend here before I come home.

I didn't get too much sleep last night as men were bringing their passes in all night long. Two men so far have been picked up by the MPs—one a corporal for being out on the street at 2:15 this morning—just 15 minutes after Saturday night curfew. The fellow may be shipped for 15 minutes carelessness. Unfair, but this is the Army. Captain Forde amuses me more every day—he's as different from Captain Stein as night from day. Just a tired old man—he wants to go home too. He's just like all of us—interested primarily in passes and furloughs.

On a typewriter it looks cold, but I love you, darling, and am just waiting for these next three weeks to pass.

With all my all, Harold

July 13, 1943
Camp Wallace

Darling,

Friday night I start cadre school. When I start to pull guard, that will be an additional evening.

I made application for my furlough.

Today I ran the battle infiltration course—with live ammunition whistling over my head. We only have to run it once, and that's plenty!

Give my love to everyone. I hope you had a good time in Wooster. I'm really getting anxious for a furlough.

With all my love, sweet, Harold

July 14, 1943
Camp Wallace

Hello Darling,

I'm enjoying the line a lot. I teach first aid classes, assist at drill, hand grenades, bayonet, and the infiltration course for which I just finished qualifying.

Cadre school started tonight. Very interesting stuff—all confidential, but worthwhile.

I think my furlough will let me leave on Monday, August 2.

Love to all, Harold

P.S. Your yank is coming—hold tight.

July 17, 1943
Camp Wallace

Lois Darling,

Received your two swell letters. Thanks a million.

Well, the impossible happened. I, as well as the other five cadremen in this platoon, am restricted for the weekend. Imagine that! Colonel Young inspected the platoon this morning and recommended restriction of the entire platoon including the cadre. So, for a dirty floor, we're all here tonight. I personally don't mind. Twenty-eight weeks in the Army—first restriction. Gig not personal, however.

One thing I'm going to do is sleep. I could use some as I've been working pretty hard.

There is talk that our Battery is going to train only schoolmen over their 4th week—and all cadre will have to be qualified to teach in telephone and radio school. If it happens, I'll leave to get off the line and go back to the office. Can't believe everything you hear. You just get settled around here and something else pops up. I'll keep my original attitude, do my best and not worry.

Love, Love, Love & more from your lonesome but hopeful soldier,

Harold

⌒

Monday, July 20, 1943
11:20 P.M.

Dearest,

I had good intentions tonight. I started to start this letter at 9:30. But "Broussard the Magnificent" came in—a very delightful bull session has been in progress. Religion, politics, sailing, ancient tortures, crimes, marriage—well, everything except the war has kept us busily engaged. He's really a top guy. Not much education, but a fine mind and a rough-and-ready tongue. Not a bad combination. After all the hypocritical politeness one hears, it's good to know a man who doesn't give a good darn what he says. I think Jack is the most interesting man I've met in the service.

The mosquitoes are awful. I've been bitten 30 times while writing this letter.

My furlough goes up to Headquarters tomorrow. I can hardly wait.

I ran the main obstacle course this P.M. Not bad—I'm getting tough again.

Tomorrow I'll go to Galveston to have dinner with our friends. Be a good girl—keep writing—say hello to the folks and Isabelle and Leon.

Love, Harold

$\backsim$

Camp Wallace
July 22, 1943

Dearest,

This has been a swell week not to be down here. Cadre school Monday, Wednesday, and Friday. CQ Tuesday, and tonight I went in an ambulance as First Aid man. So I won't have a week night off. This was unusual—two special details in one week. I guess it's true that they throw the book at you when you are about to go on furlough or/and when you come back.

Isabel is really a friend, isn't she? Time tells all.

There isn't much else to say—of course, you don't know that I love and miss you.

Be a good, patient little girl—I'll soon be on my way. Love and kisses to the folks and 3 xxx's to my girl from Texas.

Ever, Harold

$\backsim$

July 25, 1943

Hello Darling,

Lieutenant Davenport at Headquarters called me into his office to tell me he was highly impressed with the way I conducted my first aid class. He questioned me as to how long I had been assigned to C Battery, and when he dismissed me he said he was going to "see what he could do for me," whatever that may mean. Anyway, a commendation beats a gig.

Ernie (Hertzberg) phoned and wants me to go swimming with him this P.M.

I'm going to start counting the hours. How swell it will be having you back here with me after the furlough.

The heat is terrific—glad you're going to miss some of it.

Love, Harold

〰

July 27, 1943
Tuesday

Lois Dearest,

Well, you missed it. The hurricane struck! I wrote you from town and immediately returned here. At 7:30 A.M. today it hit! Galveston has an 80-mile gale and the water is hip deep down on the beach. We have no electric power and have to save water for drinking. All training stopped this noon. We're in barracks trying to keep dry. No trains are running at all so this letter won't be mailed or leave camp until the storm is over.

You can't imagine the fury of this. The wind is blowing so hard the rain goes by the window laterally. It is not yet 5:00 and it is almost dark. We'll all get plenty of sleep tonight since we'll have no lights to read by.

Just after making that last bright remark, I've been appointed in charge of a battery guard relief tonight—in case we have trouble. All I hope and pray for is that it will be cleared up in time for me to leave Sunday A.M. Bridges are down but no danger to the causeway. I'm just very thankful you're not in Galveston because no matter how much I tried, I couldn't get there now. I know now what they mean by the "storms." God, it's indescribable.

If the roads and rails are closed too long for me to leave on time, I'll let you know.

Love, Harold

〰

October 26, 1943

Dearest,

Thanks for your welcome letter.

We went out to the beach at 6 A.M. yesterday right on schedule. We fired 30 and 50 calibre machine guns all day and, after bivouacking down over night, cleaned the place up and got back at 10:30 this morning.

I may see you before you get this as I have a pretty fair chance of coming in tomorrow night. Tonight, we took a 6-mile hike with full pack. I started it with a headache, but it got better. A 6-miler with full pack & rifle is getting to be like a stroll to Wright's Drug Store to me—nothing at all!

Monday the cadre starts a pretty extensive course of study, meaning that we will be here for some time—until January anyhow.

Thursday I have to fire for record again—hard to believe it's been almost 9 months since I fired.

I had a lot of fun firing the 50 calibre machine gun. I fired a burst of about 50 rounds in just 3 or 4 seconds.

I guess I'm due for guard either Saturday or Sunday but I can't kick this week.

Well, it's almost 10:30 and I'd better get some sleep. All my love to my dearest-dearest girl in the world.

Love, Harold

⌒

October 27, 1943
Wednesday, 10 P.M.

Hello Darling,

Disappointing you tonight was one thing I had no intention of doing. We have had such a busy week—like Monday, our first bivouac. I counted on coming in tonight. We were gigged out of Wednesday nights for 2 or 3 weeks. Not only the cadre but the officers too—including Captain Forde.

Yesterday morning we were having artillery drill on the 40 guns. We were explaining all the commands pertinent to preparing the gun for action. Each platoon was operating its own gun. All of us were using the book to help explain things. All of a sudden there was General Jackson. He didn't like the idea that we used books—thought we ought to teach without them. He told Colonel Hubert and while the Colonel thought, as did our own officers, the gig was unfair and undeserved—when the General orders—we perform. So—we are going to school 5 nights a week (cadre & officers) Monday thru Friday & Saturday P.M. for 2 or 3 weeks. Then we'll be out of the dog house. I won't say it was completely undeserved. We are all rather weak on our 40s and the big shot happened along as we were soft for it.

So I'll see you weekends only for a couple of weeks—shades of the 29th! Then back to our mid-week visit. I hope to wangle the entire weekend as I fear guard again Sunday and will avoid it if possible.

Meanwhile I'll see you this weekend. Kind of rough right now—but it's a great feeling, darling, to know you're waiting for me when I get in.

> All my love, my dearest,
> Harold

~

> November 5, 1943

Dearest all,

We're getting ready for a super inspection. It was marvelous hearing your voices last night.

Here's the set-up Lois. I've contacted the B'nai B'rith in Galveston to find you a nice place to stay. May have results this weekend. Hotel rates are about $2.75 per day and no weekly rates. Must have reservation one week in advance.

Please darling, come ahead but I must know when you will arrive. I don't know how to get here as I came on a troop train.

The living situation is tough and it looks as though you'll be mostly on your own—but I definitely want you here soon.

I LOVE YOU! I LOVE YOU! I LOVE YOU!

Until we meet—just a few days more, Harold

〰

HQ Command Post
Saturday, 1:30 P.M.
November 5, 1943
Moscow, Texas

Dear Lois Darling,

Except for the fact that I miss you so much, this is almost like a vacation. The hours are long but the work is pleasant. Tell the folks that I'm OK.

It looks like I'm here for the entire bivouac. My only off hours are darkness hours and they do enforce the blackout. Will try to write again in a couple of days.

All my love to you, my one and only darling. I miss you so much.

Love and kisses,

Keep it going till Christmas day.

I Love You, Harold

P.S. You ought to see our command post (CP). Dug way into the ground—don't know it's there till you're almost in it.

〰

December 16, 1943
3:30 P.M.

Lo Darling,

My first chance to write you. It's impossible to describe this experience without actually going thru it. We have been on the go the entire time. Today is a "gas alarm" day and we've been carrying masks around all day.

It is quite a bit cooler up here than it is in Galveston, and today has

19

been drizzly and cold, much like some of those days we've had in Ohio.

Tomorrow we're supposed to move on to our second position for the last half of these maneuvers. More hard work.

I'm sleeping with Broussard and he's keeping me entertained with his perpetual good humor. This is really rough. We non-coms are on guard every other night and work all day in between.

I don't think there's much chance of my coming in early. They are so short on non-coms that while my work piles up back in the office, I'm stuck here.

I hope you'll explain to the folks why I haven't written. Dad writes the Christmas rush is big.

I love you madly—always.

Yours—with love and kisses,
Harold

January 1, 1944

It's 20 minutes to nine and I'm in charge of quarters. The Lucky Strike Hit Parade just played "I'm Dreaming of a White Christmas." A year ago tonight we sat in our little home for what we knew was the very last night—a year ago tomorrow—and I didn't dare look back. I ceased to be an average American with dreams of a peaceful future—and I became a soldier—pledged to the grim business of a war.

For what? My darling, I don't know exactly. Oh, we have no complaints. It's been a swell gypsy year. We've come to like this funny, dirty little town so far from home where we've spent the first year of this war.

I like to think I have a share in this war. It isn't much, but thinking that is all that keeps me here doing my best. For this is our war. It is our war because under our system—crazy, corrupt, comic, tragic, inefficient, slow, unfair (call it what you like), it is our only chance to have a home, dream dreams, have fun—have kids that we can educate and try to give a chance in the world.

You have a share, too. You've done a swell job so far in holding your share high. Thanks for not complaining and for taking what Uncle Sam must deal out without a whimper.

It may seem long while it goes on, but someday it will all be over and it will be as if it had never been. Then we'll have everything we ever wanted. And we'll be proud, because we fought for and proved we, like the people who built this country, have the heart and guts to fight for the things we have a right to enjoy.

Happy New Year, my darling

Harold

～

Camp Shelby
February 7, 1944
9 P.M.

Dearest,

As I am writing this you are probably in Texarkana on your way home. And believe it or not, I'm happy you're on your way—because hanging around the South waiting to come here would be wasting a lot of time. For a while, I expect to spend most of my time in the field but we hope the situation will be better in a month or two.

The situation here is absolutely nuts. This division is almost double strength now. Originally it was expected it would go overseas in January. All of us from Wallace were attached to Field Artillery battalions, but there is no room for us. Our outfit, the 881st, has a Table of Organization calling for 9 personnel clerks—when I reported it made 30 in that outfit. The same situation holds true everywhere. They are closing more camps than just Wallace (oh to be there) and are dumping non-coms into these outfits to beat the band. They want us to keep our stripes, and may even look around for some other place for us— they'll have to unless they ship their old cadre out and put us in their places which hardly sounds likely. We did get the first important break in getting into Field Artillery instead of infantry.

This is a lousy place. It's dirty, old, unattractive, huge, and rough. They use a hut instead of a barracks, sleeping 10 men to it. Comfort is sufficient but compared to our late beloved Wallace—this stinks. The food is good tho—and they have 10 movies, 30 PXs, and 5 Service Clubs—when you're on the Post.

Conclusions after one day: Oufit SNAFU. Living conditions tolerable. Chances for keeping stripes—good, if I want to go on the line. Only fair if I fight for my specialty. I fight. Chances for staying at Shelby—don't know, rather hope I can ship.

It's really too early to draw conclusions. If I'm definitely assigned to the 881st, it may not be as a clerk at first, but I can't figure out why they sent me here if they can't use me. Neither can the other hundreds of idle cadre all over the division.

New Orleans was marvelous. If I'm here long enough for you to come down we must take it in. You'll love it. I saw it with the boys— but there's no one like my best pal. We ate Trout Margery at Galatoir's.

With all my love,

From the guy who loves you best,
Harold

⤻

Camp Shelby
February 8, 1944

Dearest Darling,

Another day and no assignment. We were supposed to go out to the field today, but won't until Thursday—mainly I think because they haven't any jobs for us yet—isn't the Army nuts? We had today off and also tomorrow. I haven't done a stroke of work since I got here! Tomorrow I think I'll go to Hattiesburg and see what's what.

There are 10,000 Japanese-American soldiers here—you see them everywhere—I've met a few and they're nice boys. Don't be surprised if I have some Japanese buddies. They're smart.

They also have bowling alleys—very nice ones. In fact, if it weren't for the shanty town atmosphere, this wouldn't be a bad post.

I have been watching my watch to check on your arrival home. By now you should be there. I miss you, but can just see your mother's face, and that's compensation.

I miss you darling, but so far feel that as long as I am here—I'm glad you're safely home.

All my love & kisses to you—and please write often.

I love you,
Love to all, Harold

↜

February 9, 1944

Hello Darling,

Well, I guess tomorrow we leave for the field so they gave us 12-hour passes to Hattiesburg.

The first thing I saw when I hit here was Fine Bros-Mattison, a Kirby account. I went in to meet Milton Fine. He is a charming chap (about 40) and the first good town contact. He's also a Harvard man. Their store is another Freedlanders. We talked for about an hour.

This is a town of 35,000 and a nice clean place (not unlike Wooster). It has a very good hotel and after dinner tonight I will know more about the food. Incidentally, they give furloughs here in a hurry (since you're in the field so much) and although they're only 11 or 12 days in all, they come every 4 or 5 months. I'm due—don't get your hope raised too high, but don't be surprised if you hear the glad news soon.

Hattiesburg is a pleasant surprise, as you've probably gathered, and if I could get a garrison job here, this wouldn't be half bad. The continuous maneuvers are the only fly in the ointment. When I get to the field tomorrow (they're down at Biloxi at the Gulf) I'll know more.

Please pass this on to Wooster as it's for all of you.

All my love & kisses, Harold

↜

February 9, 1944
Saturday night

Dear Folks,

Well, I feel better now. We go definitely into the field tomorrow. And I'll find out what I'm going to do, I hope.

An amazing thing happened to me tonight. I was talking to an overseas veteran who had seen service at Guadalcanal while at the PX. He & I chatted and finally he told me he was from Wooster, Ohio. You could have knocked me over with a feather. His name is Milo Houmard and he lives at the corner of the Kidron Road beyond Riceland.

Incidentally, I'm feeling OK now. My morale is up again and I'm rarin' to go. If I don't write for a few days don't worry. But what I said when I first came in still goes. Where they want me I'll go, proudly.

Well, let Lois know I might not be able to write for a few days. Love to all, and heigh ho—I'll try to drop you all a line from the field.

Love & kisses, Harold

⌒

February 11, 1944
Monday, 10:30 A.M.

Hello Darling,

Here I am out in the field. I have been temporarily assigned to the Unit Personnel Section of the Battalion and am doing the same work I did at Wallace. They're overstaffed here and don't really need me but the Personnel Officer, Mr. Luquette (a Warrant Officer Junior Grade), would like to have me since he expects a couple of the men in this out-fit to go to the Air Corps soon. It will be up to the Battery Commander when we go in Saturday. I know I can handle the work and I think I've got a swell chance. This is a real break. We're stationed at the rear echelon, 60 miles behind the lines, and don't have to move from one place to another all the time. The fellows here are swell and if Mr. Luquette (a Warrant Officer is addressed as Mr.) likes my work, he says he can get me for Unit personnel permanently. I'll really buck for it.

This is a rainy day in the field—nothing could be more uncomfortable—but at least we're under cover. The boys at the front are not.

If this works out it will be the break I asked for. And I'll really give out with the work too. Of course, it's too early to tell yet and they've made cannoneers out of plenty of clerks, but I'm at least in a fine starting position and I'll keep pitching.

I made application for a furlough and should be home some time next month.

Love & kisses, until we write again,

Harold

P.S. Happy Valentine's Day to my Valentine.

⌐⌐

February 13, 1944
Wednesday
In the Field

Darling Dearest,

Just a few moments before dark to drop you a line—blackout tonight.

If I get the job Mr. Luquette has lined up for me I'll be very lucky. Unit Personnel is tops. The fellows here are grand. Not at all like Wallace. Included are one Harvard man, a brilliant fellow from Cleveland who is the nicest guy you ever met—nicknamed "Horrible John"—and Smitty (Earl Smith) of E. Liverpool, Ohio, already a good friend. Then there is Ritchie from Texas and one chap from Wallace still with me.

We build fires at night and last night sat up until midnight discussing politics, history, philosophy. Already I belong here. Shelby is OK. There are real people in the world after all.

I haven't heard from you yet and think there's a mixup due to our coming into the field so soon. I'm waiting for that mail. After my furlough (due soon)—I hope we can be together. There are better camps & towns by far—but never before have I met such swell people. The 881st is OK. for my money.

I miss you, sweet, and I kiss you goodnight every night.

Harold

⌐

February 18, 1944

Darling Dearest,

It's marvelous to know you're ready to come here at a moment's notice. I'm not definitely placed yet, although it looks very favorable. I may not get definite word until next week. But I have high hopes. I wouldn't think of having you come until I'm sure of being in garrison for a little while. Some of these girls stay here a month at a time while their hubbies are out in the field. I love you too much to bring you in here cold to that. I miss you terrifically but I'm glad you're home instead of waiting here while I get settled. The suspense is awful.

They are talking of issuing 3-day passes to everyone next week. I'm not sure whether new men are on the list, but if we are we won't know anything about it until we actually get our passes. Isn't that ironical? If I do get it I'll feel sick, because there isn't a chance of getting you down here in time and we go into the field immediately afterwards. I'll wire home for money and go back to New Orleans with the boys. No chance to postpone it. I'd die to have you with me but it's indefinite, the notice will be momentary, and we go out for 15 more days the week after next.

I had to laugh—you, mother, & Marvin all had to pay 3 cents to get those cards. Marvin said he's charging it to my account.

Pass this letter along to mother please—I haven't time tonight to write.

I ought to know when I get a furlough. If they push me out on the line, I'll really push hard for it—I'll have nothing to lose.

I hope you found everyone well—and give them all my love. But reserve the best of it for your own sweet self.

Love—all of it, Harold

⌒

February 22, 1944

Hello Darling,

Hyah all? We got an unexpected afternoon off so I'm dropping you a line. Glad to get your latest letter from Wooster and to know you spent a week with the folks. Let me know next time you go down and if I'm not in the field I'll phone.

You're right about my morale. It's very high. This "tough" old 1st Sergeant has become quite a pal—is urging me to try to go direct to Division Artillery HQs. It's really amazing how quickly I've gotten ahead as a new man in this organization. Of course that's always the advantage of office work. Anyhow, I'm in full charge of the Battery Office pending transfer to HQ. Yes, I'm doing swell and liking it.

A week from tomorrow back to the field for 15 days. The fightin' 69th is not so humorously known as Bolte's Bivouackin' Bastards (Major General Bolte, Division C.G.).

The weather has turned beautiful. I guess maybe Charley and I will go to Hattiesburg tonight to dine & take in a show. In the 69th there are no regular passes but you can get special passes 4 or 5 nights a week if the 1st Sergeant likes you—and mine does.

Give my love to everyone and tell them not to worry about the war—I'm now giving it all of my personal attention.

Love & kisses, Harold

⌒

February 24, 1944

Darling Dearest,

For the second time in two nights I was out of luck. Last night I called and no one answered. Tonight mother was home (I heard her voice but couldn't speak to her) and although she said to call back in a few minutes the operator told me it would be 3 hours until I could get a call-back. I'll try again.

I'm going to New Orleans on a 3-day pass tomorrow. I told the Battery Commander I'd rather wait until you get here but he said that this particular group of 3-day passes is a special gift for excellent work in the field from General M, and any future pass will depend entirely on conditions prevailing. Since I found out it won't have any effect upon another one at a later date, I'm not going to be foolish and turn it down.

Three of the boys from my outfit are going with me. Also, 3 days out of this hole will be a pleasure.

Now for a little discussion about a really important subject. Namely, your coming down. When I have a definite job, I'm classified a clerk all right but still am not in Battalion HQ. I will be able to get into Hattiesburg when in garrison almost every night.

The hotel here, the only place that looks halfway decent, is the Forrest Hotel—in Hattiesburg. It roughly resembles the Jean La Fitte, not bad, but no Buccaneer. Bus service to the post is excellent. There is supposed to be a nice Jewish Community in Hattiesburg.

A car would be advisable here. Hattiesburg is crowded with soldiers' wives who often spend considerable periods of time alone. Still they stay and manage to get by. No perfect setup you'll agree. I'm not trying to discourage you because I want you, God knows, but you'd better look it squarely in the face.

Now—if I find out in the field that I am definitely placed I'll let you know, and if I think you should come I'll remind you to wire the Forrest Hotel. Don't leave home without a confirmed reservation. The overcrowding here makes Galveston look empty. The town itself is nice—much cleaner than Galveston. Population is 35,000. One nice movie and several nice places to eat. Nothing else to do—no nite clubs—yes, one, the Swing Club, a few miles from town.

That's the story. So, stand by, love, and soon you'll get the word. I'm going to fight for transfer to higher headquarters as soon as I definitely get to Battalion.

Keep up your courage—don't lose heart—it will pass and we'll soon be where we belong—close together.

I love you with all my heart & soul. Love to everyone.

Ever & always—
Yours, Harold

⤻

New Orleans
February 25, 1944
Saturday, 3 P.M.

Hello Darling,

Just a word to let you know I've arrived.

I ate at Antoine's this noon—a most unusual place. Food wonderful. Even the bread (they serve a small loaf to each patron) is superb. I had Shrimp Antoine, Baked Chicken with Potatoes Pompano, Mocha Cake, & Coffee. Even your Dad, prime exponent of "Food- is-Food" school of thought would admit this is really something.

I got a room in a small hotel with the help of the USO (God Bless 'em). It's clean & well kept & decent—more I can not say and more I do not need.

This is a wonderful city. I'm looking forward to bringing you here. Tonight, dinner at Arnaud's (steak house). I'd rather die from overeating at Antoine's, Arnaud's, & Galatoire's than any other way I can think of. Omit the lilies—just put a Trout Margery (Galatoire's), Oysters Rockefeller (Antoine's), and Filet (Arnaud's) on my tomb. I'll be happy.

More later,
Your gourmet, Harold

⤻

Dearest Sweetheart,

It was wonderful to talk to you last night as well as to the folks.

As to this transfer—here's what I know. They are starting up a brand new Field Artillery Group, independent of the 69th. It will consist of 4 battalions of heavy guns. I have always been in a battery until I worked my way up to the next higher headquarters battalion—which I got in November at Wallace. This time, I'm going even higher. I have been selected to go on the cadre of group headquarters which is over all the battalions. It is the highest artillery headquarters (corresponding to regiment in the infantry). The advantages are several. First, chances for advancement are good. Second, privileges, such as passes and days off are more frequent. Third, the work is more interesting. Fourth, I'll be able to live off the post. It is comparable at Wallace to being moved from our orderly room in C-28 to Camp Headquarters. That's why I'm so elated. Of course, I haven't seen any orders as yet, but even though I was on pass Monday when scheduled for the interview, M/Sgt (Master Sergeant) Matthias & Mr. Luquette (WOJG) the Personnel Officer, both assure me I have made it. They wouldn't even take my laundry since I'll be transferred so soon. Tonight I washed 19 handkerchiefs. I agree with you about washing them, darling. I damn near threw them away. The transfer date is uncertain. The battalion is going out into the field tomorrow but since I'm on orders I'm being left in camp.

I think that explains things pretty well. I didn't really expect to stay here long when I discovered two things: 1) that they were impressed with the record of my work at Wallace; 2) that they had no place for me here in my classification. I have Mr. Luquette to thank for this break—he said I was too good a man to sit around and wait months for an opening. He has also urged me to take the Warrant Officer's exam when I get settled. Maybe I shall—we'll see. Anyhow, I'm in Headquarter Personnel Office Work.

Now here's a funny thing. Already the privates in this outfit are coming to me with their troubles. And I shall hate to leave them. Old "Pop" Holder, the crusty top kick, told me gruffly he "hates tuh see me go."

Keep the Olds warmed up—happy days are coming. Keep your fingers crossed and a smile on your pretty face.

Oh my God—a guy just came in and asked me to help him with his income tax! It's a great life—I love it.

But most, I adore you always,

Harold

෴

Camp Shelby, Mississippi
March 2, 1944
10 P.M.

Lo Darling,

Today was the day. My long-awaited transfer took place. At 10 this morning Mr. Luquette informed me I was on orders to "ship out" in 3 hours. At 12 o'clock, 2 hours later, General Bolte addressed the 20 of us from the 69th who were leaving and told us we were a fine cadre. At 1 o'clock, barracks bags packed and goodbyes said, we waited at the 69th HQ for the truck. It came and we left the 69th division.

We are in a peculiar position. We are activating an outfit. Twenty non-coms are the nucleus for the new 219th F.A. Group, due to activate one week from today. We 20 are the only ones in HQ Battery. No other Battery has anyone yet, not even officers. We are the guys in on the ground floor. It's a peculiar thing for me, having so recently participated in an inactivation. But tomorrow we start to work, from 1st Sergeant to Battery Mechanic, to get ready to receive our officers and trainees here in a week. I am the Battery Clerk for the Group Headquarters Battery. This time I'm starting in my own classification with a Battery of my own. That's a great break.

Another great break is to get out of the 69th. It's a rough & rugged outfit.

My "69" patches, on for just 10 days, came off tonight. I think we are to wear the insignia of the 9th Army Corps (not to be confused with 9th Service Command or 9th Army). The term "Army Corps" is broadly used to cover specialist troops doing internal (U.S.) training.

While I'm at it, I'm going to buck for an additional few stripes—this outfit suits me I think—as a training outfit. Out of 12,000 men in the 69th only 20 of us were picked. The rest of the cadre is being brought in from other posts.

Incidentally, you've probably noticed that the mail is "in care of 32nd F.A. Brigade." Since we're not activated yet, we really don't exist so our mail comes to us via them—our next door neighbors, I'll inform you when to drop that line. Anyhow—I'm tickled to death. Lucky dog me!! Knock on wood.

Gee, I miss you. I wish I could take you in my arms right now and practically crush you. I'm glad I'm getting straightened out so it won't be too many more weeks until I can have you here.

Goodnight, my lovely sweetheart.

So long—Rosebud—until tomorrow.

Ever,

Your lucky, Harold

Headquarters Battery 219th Field Artillery Group
Camp Shelby, Mississippi
March 3, 1944

Hello Darling,

You can probably tell I'm back at the old desk again by the typing and heading. This is the new outfit and not bad. It's the most unusual set up I've ever seen. We are in a HQ & HQ Battery heading an entire Group of four Battalions—in other words the controlling Battery for about 2,500 men. We have no headquarters over us so far as administration is concerned. I am a one-man personnel section. We will have just 86 enlisted men and two officers. I have my own little office, so to speak, and will have an assistant. (Gee, I'm going up in the world—until now I've usually been one). I will have charge of morning reports, and all progress charts—in other words—I am Unit Personnel. There will be ratings in this HQ eventually and I'm going to stay on the ball and try to pick one up. My 1st Sergeant is named Lattimer and he was in AA in Puerto Rico for three years before being sent back here for continental U.S. duty. He's a swell guy and 27 years old—quite a contrast to my 47-year-old top kick I left yesterday.

I can't get over the strange feeling of opening up a new unit. There will be only 20 of us here for a week or so. This area is about 4 miles from the other one where I was and is much prettier. The group head-quarters barracks have little fences and grass, and we sleep 4 to a room instead of 10 as in the 881st.

They have no permanent passes here either but are quite lenient about letting men with their wives in town go home nearly every night. Tomorrow and Sunday a lot of the boys will be sad sacks as General Marshall is coming to Shelby to make a general inspection and there will be no passes this weekend.

If our men come in pronto and all goes smoothly and settles down to the expected routine, I'll be sending for you within two or three weeks.

The poor 69th left for the field again this afternoon. Boy, am I glad I got out of "Bolte's Bivouackin' Bastards." It's rough and unpleasant.

The next two weeks will be jammed with the normal activities of getting started.

By the way, I have no idea when I'm due a furlough. The personnel officer mentioned that I'm due one but whether that means soon or late I can't tell yet. I am not in position to press hard for one right now but will ask as soon as I'm sure I'm not jeopardizing this deal.

I'm not kidding myself that I haven't walked into my toughest assignment, but I know all the work so well it's just a question of organizing my time to get it out and I can do that. And I'm close enough to brigade headquarters here and to the Group Headquarters too (this is Group HQ Battery) to be able to step in there to a higher rating.

That's about all for now from your Mississippi mud turtle (I guess for a long time to come, but I can think of worse places).

Love and kisses to everyone, but most and always most of all to my darling.

Your, Harold

〜

Headquarters Battery 219th Field Artillery Group
Camp Shelby, Mississippi
March 5, 1944

Darling Dearest,

Sunday on an Army Post! This is YOUR Army hour coming direct from the as yet non-activated and non-existent organization so proudly emblazoned on the letterhead. You will notice this is not a lowly battery, or an almost as lowly battalion, but a group headquarters—I remind myself of the guy who ran away in the heat of battle and headed for the rear. He finally pulled up to salute what he thought was a lieutenant, no a captain, no a major, no a colonel, no, by God, it was a Major General. In amazement he said, "I had no idea I'd run that far!" I've run that far—in our Group Headquarters. I am a considerable distance from the line now—having started with a 40 mm battery at Wallace a little over a year ago.

This new job of mine is no sinecure and no snap. I shall have to work like the devil at it. We are a separate battery with no battalion connections, being in a higher unit than battalions (there will be seven new battalions of field artillery under this Group) so I am a one-man unit personnel section all by myself. It will be a little rough at first but eventually when I get an assistant trained it will be OK. I'm allowed one of the T/O (Tables of Organization, the Bible, and open-sesame to everything the Army has). Meanwhile I shall take care of service records, payroll, and everything else of a personnel nature for 100 enlisted men and about 16 officers. I have never handled officers' personnel work before, but it can't be much different from anything else—just follow the regulations.

We got passes after all for Saturday night only, so last night I went into Hattiesburg. Bus service to camp is bad and the only thing we can do to spend a decent part of the evening together is to have a car and I'll drive back and forth. All I'm waiting for now is to get a little start on my new job before taking off most every night (by the way, I probably won't get in every night) and I also want to make quite sure they don't decide to assemble us here and train us at Fort Sill, Oklahoma. We shall have to wait for all this to straighten out. This new job of mine is far more extensive than anything else I've ever handled. and I'm going to be on my own practically all the time, so naturally I'll have to start in high gear.

If I had my way you'd be here now. I've missed you "something fierce" as the natives would say. In about two weeks from now if all goes well I'll make a reservation for you at the hotel.

There isn't much more except to tell you again and again that I love you. Absence does make the heart grow fonder. I know I've got just about the swellest girl in the world and I'm getting hungry to be with her. I guess I'm just no good without you—I eat, sleep, drink a beer or two, and work and get up the next day to do the same thing over again—no interest, no glamour, no nothing. I need you and feel, even for these next few weeks until I have you again, that the only hardship in the Army that will ever mean a thing to me is not to be close to you. I think when this damned war is over, you and I will go up to the north woods and deliberately get snowed in for about 6 months. Maybe I'm silly, because we are so very lucky, but I know this—they can have the two little stripes I've got, and anything else they want, as long as they let me keep you with me.

Incidentally, speaking of stripes, there is a possibility I may get another one some day not too many years off. In miniature, I'll be doing a Tec/Sgt's work at Corporal's pay, but they may give me a boost a month or two after activation. Don't hold your breath or go out to buy chevrons.

That's about all. Isn't there a birthday or something in your family this month? Put me wise, honey.

Write me a nice long sugar report—I need it. And start to think of being a camp-follower again. If you don't come when I call you, I'll have to come all the way to Cleveland and carry you back personally.

All my love and kisses to you darling, forever. Give my love to the folks. Why don't you have mother drive down here with you when you come?

All My Love, Harold

⌣

Headquarters Battery 219th Field Artillery Group
Camp Shelby, Mississippi
March 6, 1944

Hello Darling,

I got a real break tonight. I am pulling my first charge of quarters and about 5 minutes ago it started raining cats and dogs. So instead of getting caught at the PX or the movies here I am snug and dry in the orderly room for the night.

In just a couple of days we'll know what the score is. Tomorrow the Colonel is due in (he's Group commander) and by Wednesday practically all the officers (there will 22 assigned to the headquarters staff) will be here. Thursday and Friday the enlisted men start to come in. Of course, at 0001 (one minute after midnight) Thursday A.M. the 9th, we activate and a brand new Field Artillery group will be born—seven combat battalions under us. Most of the privates are transfers from Coast Artillery and even some of the battery officers scheduled to come in in the lower echelons are CAC. I wonder if I'll have any friends among them. The reason for all this transferring from CAC to Field Artillery is that the United Nations are definitely off of the defensive and on to the offensive from now on in. No longer is there danger of any more than a morale raid on our shores. Enemy planes are too hard pressed to risk even that, probably, and if they did the damage they could do in a few raids it would be less important to us than the loss of their planes would be to them. Consequently the anti-aircraft installations in this country are being cut to the bone and maintained as a thin protective cover at vital spots only—naturally just where they are being maintained is military information. The Texas Gulf Coast is definitely not one of the places.

Experience of the British, the Russians, and our own troops has proven that this war will not be won in the air alone. It will be won by infantry taking the ground and holding it. The battle of Italy is partic-ularly difficult because not everywhere can armored columns and tanks break thru the Hun defenses—on the beachhead at Cisterne, and in the mountains 70 miles away at Cassino, our Armored Divisions have been unable to make much headway. Why? Because when the enemy is well entrenched as the Germans are in Italy and the terrain favors defense, as it does there, ground must be won foot by foot. This means the foot troops have to advance a yard at a time—rather remi-niscent of the trench warfare of World War I which we thought out-dated but which is by no means so—given a determined opposition and favorable ground. So what happens? We find we have concentrat-ed on airplanes, tanks, armored forces, anti-aircraft, chemical warfare, and to a lesser degree on the greatest "tough war" combination in the business—infantry supported by hard smashing field artillery. If we had enough batteries of 105s and 155s (howitzers, in other words sawed-off cannon) to drop shells right among the Germans 24-hours-a-day 7-days-a-week they would not be able to hold even the most dif-ficult positions. But I'm afraid exactly the reverse has been nearer the truth over there. It is the enemy who has the "long Toms" and the howitzers and our infantry is at a disadvantage. So, although the situation is being improved as fast as possible, the General Staff realizes that in order to fight this static close—combat infantry—artillery team warfare we need more infantry divisions supported by heavier, deadlier artillery. One thing is true: we could have made a far better showing in Italy had General Clark been willing to sacrifice men like the Russians or Germans, or even the British, do. But America is trying her damnedest to make every man count and literally will not undertake an operation if waiting might save even one small patrol. Therefore the advance has been held up until we accumulate an arsenal of Field Artillery over there that will not be able to be stood up to. That won't be us. Those boys are probably on the way already. But since the fact has been proven, they don't want to get caught short again. So it's "Hi Hi Hee, for the Field Artillery" as they said in 1917— when the same thing was true. That is why AA and Coast Artillery Corps officers and men are being transferred literally in droves to the Field Artillery.

Enough of the art of war which is fascinating but not half as much so as you are. I got your two sweet letters. By the way, my address is now completely permanent.

When I get out of this thing, and even before, I'm not going to worry too much about anything—it doesn't pay. My chief aim in life, and the thing I have always had in mind, is your happiness, and I'm not ashamed to tell you that being in love with you is my main business—now and always. Of course I have to have a job and I expect to be a success at it. I guess it takes participation in a war to realize what the real values are.

It won't be long now until I'll have everything all set at this end for you to come down—once we get the first couple weeks after activation out of the way and everything is going smoothly.

Do you remember Joe Berini, the cook from C-28? He came here with me but I didn't see him after we got here because he was sent to another outfit in the 69th. Well, he made this new cadre too, and we are living in the same room together. Joe is anxious to have dinner with us. He's a swell guy, a Swiss with a rather charming accent. Poor Charley Thomas is definitely in the Infantry and is out in the field now. The 69th will be out until the 18th and back in until April 1st when they go out again for 2 months. Praise the Lord and pass me some wood to knock on—literally "out of the woods" on that deal.

Not speaking personally at all, this is a crack cadre. They picked it very carefully and that is a compliment to us all. After all, there isn't a man in the 69th who wouldn't have liked it, not only to remove that APO from his address, but because a training cadre is the best deal. We thought at first our men would be new recruits. It appears, however, they have completed 13 weeks basic and will start on the long grind of unit training. Some of the battalions may have basics among them. The funny thing will be these CAC officers who know their 40s and 90s but don't know a thing about the field pieces. They'll have to learn right with the men, bars or no bars.

Hope you're feeling better. Take good care of yourself—after all, you're mine and I want you in A-1 condition! Tell your private doctor I want him to render me a bill for his services. After all, it's not fair to take his daughter from him then give her back temporarily just for medical treatment.

My God, this letter has just gone on and on. I am happiest when talking to you, so I hate to quit and since I now can type them again, I don't get writer's cramp.

Did I tell you, Jack Broussard sent his love to you? He's a great guy, and the only fellow from Wallace that I have any intention of corresponding with. Separation makes you find your friends—too close contact day after day obscures your judgement.

Give my love to everyone—I'm writing to Mother tomorrow night.

All my love to my sweetheart—I'm counting the days until I can send for you.

Your, Harold

Darling,

This was the day! We activated at 8 o'clock this morning. No ceremony or anything like that—one minute we were nothing and the next we were in existence—the Headquarters of the 219th Field Artillery Group, attached to the IX Army Corps, Special Troops, came into existence as a component part of the Second Army. If that isn't quite clear to you I'll explain it later. There has been so much red tape today (although red tape is my business and keeps me from getting into worse trouble) that I'm a little tired of the Army tonight. I can't even type straight.

Our new B.C. is one swell guy. He is a captain named Philbeck and he made a very fine impression on all of us. He called us all in—told us there were plenty of ratings to be had in this baby outfit, that we could get anything we wanted by putting out for him and playing fair and, most important for me, that married men, if their wives came down, would have complete off-duty passes seven nights a week (of course, excepting unusual cases of extra work). We're all for him and I never saw such high morale in a cadre as we have here. I went down to Finance today and met Miss Ross (a civilian) who is going to check our payrolls and get everything straight so I can arrange to pay these guys soon. Camp Shelby looks pretty good to me at this point and I think this is the best deal yet. There may be ratings soon and it is entirely possible I may be pulled up into Group Headquarters (I think Colonel Casale would like me there) and the only reason I'm not there now is that Captain Philbeck told the Colonel he needs me here. So, what do I care?

I went to town last night to see about the Forrest Hotel. Their prices are the same as the Buccaneer's for singles but they do not allow anyone to double up by the night. A double room runs from $3.85 to

$5.50. If it is comfortable and nice I wouldn't mind paying $120.00 a month for a while and find something else because we shall be Mississippians for quite a while.

We should be straightened out here around April 1st and that is the time I think you should come. Try to arrange your schedule so as not to arrive on a weekend. Does that sound OK to you? I'm just so damned anxious to have you here I get all excited when I think about it. Some people may not like it, and it is not Galveston, but it does have its points and we can be together. There is a very nice guy in our cadre from Worcester, Massachusetts, named Sam Babbitt—a landsman. He seems OK and if his wife comes from Worcester that is a better lead to an Army couple than any I had at Wallace in 13 months. The fellows I knew in the 881st are already history.

I can't think of much else, except I miss you and am counting the days until I have you here. Please write to me often. I guess some letters went astray. Give my love to everyone and especially Mother and Dad. Have your pop brush you up on your drawl—you all's comin' to the deep South, honey-chile.

Love and kisses, Harold

〜

March 12, 1944

Darling,

Here it is Sunday morning and I am up at the ungodly hour of 8:30. I am on CQ today since I am trying to pull a few weekend duties before you come. Then the decks will be cleared for awhile.

Everything is going along fine. We are still in the preliminary stages. In setting up my little section I need a stapler, a hole-punch, and some metal Acco fasteners which the Post Quartermaster hasn't got and I don't know what in the hell I'm going to do without them. Regulations prescribe using staples to fasten a payroll but without any I can't do it. We have an A priority for all metal office supplies but they are really scarce. I'll have to ask the B.C. for a pass to Hattiesburg to pick the stuff up at a civilian store—black market if necessary.

The officers are swell in this outfit. I had a chance to try out for Message Center Chief (Sergeant) but it's work I never had and under the setup here I think I'll stick to unit personnel for awhile. Our original 20 EM has been increased to 22 now, and we have 61 men scheduled to come in the 24th. I am the only man exempt from KP—even the 1st Sergeant is pulling it today. I will pull a lot of CQ's, however, as with my many and varied duties (Battery Clerk, unit personnel, mail clerk for the moment) I haven't time to pull KP or latrine orderly. When a cadre is all you've got, it makes a difference, and we all have to work together to get organized. I went down to Finance yesterday to get all the dope on the payroll and had a long talk with a WAC sergeant. This post has an easier payroll system than Wallace had and I like the Finance Department very much.

We know a little more about this outfit now. We are the Group Headquarters (in battle known as the Rear Detachment Headquarters). When we get our filler replacements in we will be 94 enlisted men and 21 officers. This will be the "General Staff" of this outfit. Under us will be 7 battalions of Field Artillery—about 6,000 men and 200 officers. We will train here at Shelby and the unofficial and wholly unconfirmed story is that we will be here a year or more. Our men are coming mostly from Coast Artillery, although being in a headquarters now, I probably won't see as much of the actual work of the batteries and battalions on the line.

The more I see of this chap Babbitt the better I like him. I think all of us will get along fine—he's the life of the party and as good a guy as you'd want to meet.

Joe Berini of Wallace is anxious to meet you again. He is rather lonesome down here and we'll have to have dinner with him. I still can't get used to being in on the ground floor in my own job.

I'll be waiting for the word as to exactly when you expect to get here.

Colonel Casale (Lt. Col. Ex. Officer) commended me on the first morning report—said it was "an excellent job." He's a very neat, precise, man—and a very good exec.

Give my love to everyone, and for the next three weeks I'll be counting the hours. Maybe a month from today we'll be in New Orleans. It's only three hours from Hattiesburg and we can take a lot of week-end trips to break the monotony of Mississippi. All my love and kisses to my darling sweetheart.

Ever, always, and only,
Yours, Harold

P.S. I asked Captain Philbeck, the B.C., about the pass situation. Married men living off the post will have off-duty passes at all times. This time I'm going to commute rations and collect 67 cents a day from Uncle Sam for food. Then I'll eat only my noon meal on the post for 25 cents and be in the clear 42 cents a day—three packs of cigarettes. I think we shall start here pretty much as we finished at Wallace. The hours will not be quite so good, but what the hell? The boss is opening up shop a little earlier, that's all.

Love and kisses,
Devotedly, Harold

Headquarters Battery 219th Field Artillery Group
Camp Shelby, Mississippi
March 12, 1944

Hello Darling,

Two letters in one day—I must be in love. I just figured that since I'm still on CQ and am "stuck" here in the office tonight, I couldn't do anything better than whisper a few sweet nothings in your ear.

I just remembered you asked about clothes. The natives tell me that it's going to get plenty hot. We've had an unusually cold February and March for Mississippi and everybody expects it to get very warm. For

Hattiesburg sport clothes definitely are best. Our society will be the friends we make—mostly Army people.

This Babbitt chap I've talked about makes a better impression on me every time I see him—which is almost continually. He has a lot of vitality. He's been in Shelby quite a while and his wife was down before when he was in the 69th and they had trouble finding people they really liked so that sounds encouraging. Discriminating people, as a rule, are looking for the same thing. He's a right guy—gets along with everyone.

By the way, I got into a poker game last night (see what happens when you're not around to take up my time) and lost twenty bucks. I just get bored doing nothing and had rotten luck. Could you send me a postal money order for twenty-five? I'm a little hard-pressed and though I could borrow money I'd rather not. Thanks for the check—and please, God, make these next three weeks fly by so you'll get here and keep me out of trouble or I'll probably get in another game and lose my shirt again. I'm not really fond of gambling but there is so little to do and you can't read all the time.

I'll kiss you goodnight and tuck you in—soon I'll be doing just that again. I'd like to give the calendar a push.

I love you with all my heart,

Harold

꙳

Headquarters Battery 219th Field Artillery Group
Camp Shelby, Mississippi
March 19, 1944

Hello Darling,

The war is looking better, especially in the Pacific. Progress seems slow, but those 4,000 miles to Tokyo don't mean as much as they seem to, when you realize that actual land fighting is possible only at intervals spaced hundreds of miles apart. The Japanese fleet has met its master in the United States Navy and knows it. Imagine what additional punch will be thrown into the Pacific war when large units of the British fleet are thrown in there after Europe cracks. As to Europe, the only worries seem to be diplomatic. We are definitely scoring a tremendous victory in the air over the Reich. In Italy, we are moving ahead very slowly, but in military axiom, any invading army that keeps on going is winning. Some day Germany will have expended all she dare in Italy and it will crack down there all at once. The Nazis are making their big stand, as all German armies have always done, on foreign soil. The chances are they won't be so anxious to bloody up every mile of the Fatherland. But the RAF and our own Eighth Air Force are doing a good job of that.

The magnificent advances of the Russians are proving the wisdom of their heroic stand a year ago at Stalingrad and two years ago before Moscow. Militarily, Hitler is by no means thru, but soon he must commit his reserves somewhere, and since he will be shorter on that valuable commodity than we are, once they are committed he is open to blitz himself. I don't blame the Russians for feeling we are trying to save American and British lives by delaying the second front until we have nearly worn out the enemy with Russian victories. But, I, as a soldier, cannot say that we in the Army do not appreciate the General Staff's solicitude.

Diplomatically, it is another story. We are now in a position where we have no foreign policy at all as regards the Balkans, and no definite policy regarding Italy that makes any sense. We, with the British, have supported the "little king" and Badoglio (the butcher of Ethiopia) but never accorded them recognition. Now the Soviet government takes the lead in recognizing these arch Fascists and we are neither for nor against it. A bad spot. I think "Jedge" Cordell Hull had better get on the ball or get out. The old game of power politics is being played again, and it's very discouraging. I don't think the American or British people want it played—I'm not sure the governments want to. It seems to me that the only way to avoid it is to set up military governments in conquered countries that are strictly temporary and let each individual people decide for itself what it wants to do. After the war we will be sure of democracy in only six European countries—all small ones— Switzerland, Denmark, Norway, Sweden, Holland, and Belgium. They are thoroughly soaked in democracy and will undoubtedly go right back to it. France, where we have spurned de Gaulle, the peoples' obvious choice, is uncertain; Czechoslovakia, sold out at Munich, will be a democracy with her face toward mother Russia; and the rest of Europe looks like a nightmare now. Russia has no intention, in spite of Cairo and Teheran, of permitting small nations to have their say, and her treatment of Poland and the Baltic states seems to indicate she will tolerate no interference from the two Western democracies (U.S. and Britain). The Atlantic Charter was murdered by Churchill when the British government decided to allow the White Paper in Palestine to go into effect the 31st of this month, barring Jewish immigration and sacrificing Zionism which Britain herself supported, to the exigencies of Arabian politics (and Arabian oil). Even the United States has refused to protest against the sellout of Palestinian Jews. The Army says it would be unwise to interfere with British policy in the Near East at this time, but I personally don't think the Army gives a damn. I think we are interested in contracts in Saudi Arabia for pipe lines and King Ibn Saud has demanded a hands-off policy on Palestine as his price for giving concessions to American oil interests after the war. I'm no Zionist but the need for a refuge for millions of European Jews is so apparent that no one who opposes Zionism for them can have a heart at all. So once again, our people are being sold down the river for imperialist interests. I'm sure the U.S. government is not proud of her lack of guts on this issue, but we will need that oil as a leverage to our own powerful position in the post-war world. We as Jews should surely not rejoice when this cheap oil comes pouring in. We will be driving our cars after the war, so to speak, with the blood of our brothers rather than gasoline. There is nothing as good Americans that we can do that Rabbis Wise and Silver did not do two weeks ago in Washington. Those poor devils in Europe, after all they have gone thru, have very little to look forward to in an Allied victory.

There is a bright side, tinted Red. The peoples of Central Europe are turning more and more towards Russia as they see we have no policy for them. The great prestige of America in Europe has waned, and in its place Russia has stepped in. Totalitarian as she is, the U.S.S.R. is rapidly progressing toward at least lip service for freedom. Perhaps what we cannot do, or are unwilling to do, in the old country, the Russians will be ready and willing to do.

Enough of the "Review of the Week." At this point all that you can get out of it is confusion. What I want, frankly and unashamedly, is you. This much I can see—my interest in everything else hinges on that. I can be interested in politics, history, and everything else, as long as you are near. When you're not, I have to drive myself to keep up. All is not right with the world when you're not here and I sort of function on one cylinder. So at the moment, and until you get here, I am waiting—just waiting. Thank God it won't be long now.

Give my love to the folks and tell them I'll take good care of you down here. Most of all, love to my dearest, always.

Your, Harold

⌒

Headquarters 219th Field Artillery Group
Camp Shelby, Mississippi
April 6, 1944

Darling,

This, we are told, is Army Day. On this day, just 27 years ago, President Wilson asked for and got a Declaration of War against the Imperial German Government which we thought was pretty brutal, but which was civilized compared with the present gangsters.

I hope you had a good time in Wooster. I'm sure Mother enjoyed having you down. We finally got orders on our men—30 of them are coming this weekend from Fort Benjamin Harrison Indiana Reception Center, and 10 more from Wilmington, Delaware ASTP School (washouts). That will still leave us 20 men short but they should be along soon. Anyway, I shall almost certainly have a May furlough.

Thanks for the clippings from the Record. I see that Myles Beeler finally went. I'm glad Tom Landes is getting a break—he's a good guy and probably was wasted at Hayes almost as much as I was at Wallace. Gee, there isn't anybody left in Wooster.

The news of the past 10 days has not been very significant except for the continued Russian advance toward Odessa. Soviet operations, as well as our air war, are progressing according to plan. The greatest story of the past week was Mr. Wilkie's announcement last night at Omaha that he is not a candidate. He stood for the only truly liberal element in the G.O.P. and with his passing from Republican leadership, the party falls back to the die-hards, isolationists, and America Firsters who almost wrecked this country and played coy with the Fascists. If Dewey or anyone like him such as Bricker (perish the thought) gets the nomination, the old wheel horses that speak for reaction and no real peace will control him. This also practically assures the President of a fourth term since no one of Wilkie's intellectual calibre can be found to combat him. And Wilkie himself, disgusted with the machine politics that beset him and interested only in spoils and not the least in really winning the peace, may bolt the Republican party and form a third one. If he does, we'll have a repetition of 1912 when Teddy Roosevelt broke off from the G.O.P. to form the Bull Moose party and pulled enough votes away from Taft to elect a Democrat—Woodrow Wilson. The wheel has turned again. The long-run effect is bad. We need a two-party system to preserve democracy, and if the Republicans are repudiated once more by the people, there will be only one party with any national control.

Even though I am a Democrat, I want to see a strong Republican opposition for the sake of free politics. Undoubtedly a third party will arise. Maybe Wilkie will head it. If he gets the right kind of liberals—like Burton of Ohio, Ball of Minnesota, Hatch of New Mexico, Voorhees of California—maybe I will switch to his side. The old party bosses of Republicanism are as corrupt and unpatriotic as ever—they don't deserve anyone's confidence—at least not a liberal's anymore.

This letter was just interrupted by lunch after which we had a mixed volleyball game—officers and EM. Lots of fun—these officers are certainly a swell bunch.

After what you wrote concerning fellows overseas. I guess we can wait until furlough for that big hello. I do miss you terribly—when you're not here most of me is missing. Until then I'll dream of you every night and think of you every day. Because I think you're just about the best thing that ever happened. I love you from the bottom of my heart.

Regards to the folks.
Ever,
Your, Harold

⌐⌐

Headquarters Battery 219th Field Artillery Group
Camp Shelby, Mississippi
April 10, 1944

Darling,

Just got your last letter from Wooster. Glad to hear that you had a good time. I know mother did.

I spent Saturday night with Sam and Nat Babbitt—they insisted on my staying over at their apartment. I had a very pleasant time and Sunday afternoon, on my way back, I stopped in the USO and sat down at the piano for a minute (I thought) but played for 3 hours—had quite a gang of guys gather round and lots of fun—the most I've had in town. So instead of getting into camp early, I got home about 8. It was lots of fun, and some of the fellows want me to come back next Sunday P.M.

Our men are due momentarily, but have not appeared as yet. But this month-long period of waiting for them will soon be over. Captain Philbeck said he will try to start furloughs as soon as possible. This is happening as I feared—we'd hold off waiting and the men's arrival would drag, as it has, for almost three weeks now. I'll believe they're coming when I see them. I hope it isn't fall before they get here—because we will not get furloughs before they come and are classified. This is the only subject when my blood pressure goes up. There you are up in Ohio, but this damned delay has to hold us up. If this goes on much longer I shall just have to have you come down and have my furlough postponed.

This is probably getting monotonous for you—every letter the same ineffective complaint. It happens to be, however, most of my thinking at the moment so you might as well know it. If I knew we had a year here, or more, I wouldn't say a word. These people who just moved from Wallace together were smart after all. This is war, and there's no time for much planning.

Take good care of yourself, dear.

I feel fine, and don't worry. I just get mad sometimes, and I'm not trying to take it out on you—it's just nothing else in the world matters to me.

Ever,

Your, Harold

⌒

November 9, 1944

Darling,

I arrived in camp tonight—pausing in Hattiesburg just long enough to catch the bus. The trip down was uneventful and I ate my three "meals" and talked with my fellow victims who were southward bound. I got a funny twinge today when I recognized parts of the road we had driven but they were glorious days.

We were an hour late—not that I cared. I arrived here exactly twenty-four hours after leaving Cincinnati Union Station. The only mail awaiting me was a letter from Mother.

News! First rain in these parts for over a month.

I intended to work tonight but I'm dog tired so I shall clean my shoes then hit the hay.

There is plenty of work piled up here for me and I think I shall celebrate my birthday working. We started working every other night so I'm just as happy about your being home. I think it has been a glorious thing that we were able to be together for so long.

I hope you had a pleasant trip home. I appreciate your self-control—I had all I could do to hold back. I'm secure in our love and happiness is never absent when we are separated—I know you are going to think of me as I am of you, constantly.

Tomorrow I have a huge stack of work and a payroll to make out. I can't close without a whoop of joy over the election. It looks as though Ohio deserted the victory column though. That finishes Tom Dewey for the present, and Ham Fish and Gerald Nye too—and we'll be very grateful.

The rain is coming down hard now. The first of the seasonal storms.

Give my love to the folks—Terry, Joe, and Leo send their love.

And I send all of mine to you, darling.

Ever yours, Harold

Mobile, Alabama
November 12, 1944

Darling,

After talking to you yesterday, we came here. The boys had a wonderful time and so did I. They used the Coast Guard orchestra which is pretty good, and dancing continued until 1 A.M. An old man like me can hardly take it any more. They put the boys up at the USO but when we first got here, I went out and got a room at a small hotel so I had private quarters. This morning I had breakfast at the Admiral Semmes, and then came back to the USO to write and wait for the boys to get dressed and eat—we'll leave for camp about 12:30.

This was the day I promised you a complete news-letter. First, the re-election of the President has been a terrific boost to allied morale outside the U.S. Regardless of how sincere Governor Dewey may have been, his election and the defeat of the President would certainly have been regarded as repudiation by the people of our war effort. Similarly the Axis powers, now desperate, would have taken some comfort from the defeat of their mortal enemy F.D.R. so the results have been a great help to our friends and a hard blow to our enemies.

Second, it now seems clear that immediately following the war, there will be only two great powers left in the world—Russia and the U.S. The British Empire will be divided internally to such a large extent (ex. India) that it will be impossible for her to show a firm voice at the peace table or afterwards. France is a small nation—she will be loved and protected by her allies of 150 years, but not feared. China, torn by a war more destructive than any nation has ever had to endure, and split between Chiang and the Communists, will be slow to recover. I believe that eventually she will take her place beside us and the U.S.S.R. Until the wounds of war and civil strife heal and her industrialization is completed, she will be the sleeping giant. So we will see the phenomenon of a world whose power will be largely concentrated in two capitals—Washington and Moscow. London will be very important but she will never again rate with the giants and her greatness will depend on the cooperation she received from us and the Bolshevists. Take the conference about air regulations; Washington and Moscow want freedom of the air—London originally proposed national air "highways" after the war.

The next two powers in line, China and France, waited until they saw which way the wind blew—then came to our point of view. This war will mark our entry into world politics as the greatest power on earth along with the Soviet. Isolation is not only dead—it lies buried and un-honored under our emergence on the stage in a position held in the past by Greece, Rome, Spain, and the British Empire. Our age has dawned. May we be wise enough to merit the position for many generations.

Take good care of yourself and write often. I live for your letters. I also am living for the day when I can change clothes and come home.

All my love to the folks—and even more to you, my dearest

Ever yours, Harold

P.S. As I finished this, a little sailor sitting opposite me here in the writing room asked me how to spell "jealous." I'm glad I don't have to use that word.

〜

November 13, 1944

Hello Darling,

I've been busy around here—not a moment to let up. That's a good thing, because it gives me very little time to feel sorry for myself.

I know it's hard to be patient when your world seems to slip out from under you, but the main thing we have to do now is to fight with ourselves—for patience and understanding. We can't really get it from civilians and if we don't have inner strength it will be twice as hard as is necessary. After all, this is the greatest event that is going to happen in our time, and there does come a time when all you can do is bow before the storm. I am quite able to take care of myself and therefore there is no cause for any worry in my line.

Don Lundsgaard, the chap you met one evening, just got back from furlough. The first thing he spotted was my wedding ring and he said, "Lois isn't so dumb." He was met by a superior smile, I can assure you.

My day is full of questions—how about this, and that, how do I send money home to my mother, brother, sister, wife, grandma, aunt, etc. I never stop from the moment I set my foot in the door. I greet one and all with the same courteous, "Well, what in hell do you want?". I have been working alone since I came back, but now that Lundsgaard is back, I shall be able to get the work out. The Inspector General arrived yesterday. He hasn't got horns and seems like a nice guy. He can't restrict me anyhow—I'm not going anywhere.

So far, no change in departure date. Still after December 1st as originally planned. We are already getting set for three-day passes from POE. Keep your fingers crossed. There will be fifty thousand wives down there. I'll give you the word when the time comes.

Thanks again for your sweet letters, and so—goodnight Snooks.

Love, Harold

⌇

Camp Shelby, Mississippi
November 16, 1944

Snooky Darling,

This was a busy day. Jerry Grimaldi is in here bothering the hell out of me and I can't concentrate. Things seem to be very confused especially getting the work out. Nobody knows what we are doing. Shipping date has not changed.

Everyone is on edge—tonight we finish packing cargo equipment and ship it off. Then we wait.

I'm making out a $35.00 allotment effective January first. You should get your first check around the 10th of February and every month thereafter.

A band is playing retreat but for me it's just the beginning. I have hours of work tonight. I'll be glad when I get Lundsgaard trained.

Well, that's about all for now. Take good care of yourself. Regards and love to everybody.

Ever yours with hugs and kisses,

Harold

⌇

November 18, 1944

Hello Darling,

Just got your letter and I'm happy again. Seems all I do is wait for them.

Well, this time I'm out of the office for good. I've got Lundsgaard well broken in and McCarthy just got back from Texas. Finally I can concentrate on message center. After a 2-month absence, I'll have plenty of work to do. We have very little time left in Mississippi, probably just a couple more weeks.

It certainly seems as though something is wrong with Hitler. He may be dead, but I don't think that's particularly important at this point. More important is the big offensive which seems to be opening up on the Western front. Maybe it will end this winter. Perhaps the 219th can fire a little stuff into Germany first.

Yesterday noon I worked right thru the lunch hour so I went into the mess hall and Joe broiled me a steak. He's a good egg.

As my loneliness for you grows, my hatred of our enemies increases. Perhaps we never learn to hate until we are deprived of what we want. I want you—and now I can hate.

All the gang sends love,

Ever,
Your, Harold

November 23, 1944

Hello Darling,

This being Thanksgiving we got 1/2 day holiday.

We had a wonderful turkey dinner with all the fixings and Joe cooked it himself—it just melted in our mouths.

I'm thinking of all the Thanksgivings we've spent together (Joe cooked our last Thanksgiving dinner at Camp Wallace, remember?) and praying we will be eating the next one together. We shall someday be able to take up our lives where we left them on November 1—forever and forever together. That's what I'm fighting for—my war aim.

With all my love, Harold

P.S. My love to everyone—tell Mom & Pop I'm thinking of them.

Sweetheart Darling,

What little I have read leads me to believe that the Germans are going to take a hell of a beating, but will probably hold out until the Spring offensive. Himmler (I believe Hitler is either dead or insane) has a pistol at the back of the German Army and although the Germans are trying desperately to negotiate with us thru neutrals, it doesn't seem likely Britain, Russia, or the U.S. will be tricked into giving the Huns a compromise peace. The fighting on the Western front will continue bitter and relentless, never letting up, until one day in late winter or early spring it will be all over.

The Japs, on the other hand, are really just beginning to fight. They have lost their island empire in the South Pacific. But they hold China in a stranglehold and it will take more than B-29 raids to break it. Probably the plan is to take Korea, Formosa, and the main China ports, and then to force an entrance onto Honshu or other Japanese islands. If successful, it will be up to the Chinese to regroup and chase the Japs out of Manchuria and the central provinces of China. I don't think we shall do much continental fighting in China. Obviously, this is not a short nor easy job. The War Department is very concerned over the slackening effort in the ammunition factories, and no doubt that has been a factor in causing the battle on the Western front to go slowly. Now that Secretary Hull is out, we may see a bolder foreign policy to Argentina. Whatever the case may be, we shall be citizens of the most powerful nation in the world when this is over.

Love to all of you.

I love you, Harold

Dear Folks,

This is not the regular Sunday letter, but an attempt to get everything ready for Lois' arrival.

When you arrive in Galveston, honey, inquire at the bus station for Camp Wallace. It is across the street from the Jean La Fitte hotel where I have a reservation. Take the bus to Camp Wallace. The MPs (Military Police) may ask you for identification and reason for coming to the entrance of the military reservation. Tell them you have a reservation at the guest house which they will call and confirm. Bring your small bag only to camp. Do NOT bring a camera on the reservation.

When you get to the guest house they will get in touch with me. If I draw KP it may be late, but I'll see you Friday night. We have tough inspections on Saturday and all day Sunday.

My duties are getting stiffer. I am going to eventually get a chance at O.C.S. That means close attention to work.

The Army is unpredictable. We'll never know when a date will stick—but we'll be close and should get weekends and at least 1 or 2 other nights a week.

I hope, Mother and Dad, you come down next month. Please, please do.

I've been so excited I forgot to write Mother Rubin on her birthday and I got a lovely letter from her.

Well, in 5 days I'll see you, baby. Never for long, but often.

All My Love, Harold

P.S. Clothes: Dress for Ohio in April. You may need a summer dress and a pair of good slacks to sit around the lobby with other Army wives, a light spring coat and one good black dress. Two good stores here—E.S. Levy and Cohen Co. Prepare to read, write, knit, and wait—the code of the Army wives. That will be 98% of your life.

Love you, Harold

⌣

Hello Sweetheart and Everyone,

Probably the last letter from Camp Shelby "Mississloppy."

We've been working day and night for a week—every time I took a pass, I paid for it in overtime. Boy, it's rough.

The main purpose of this letter, since I can't write anything else, is not to worry if you don't hear from me for several days. Just stand by, and keep writing. I'll get your letters eventually.

This has been a week of retrospect for me. The end of my first phase—camp life in the U.S. It has fortunately been a long period—far longer than I had any right to expect—a year ago I anticipated the end of it—but was lucky enough to have almost another year with you, dear. It has been so wonderful, I can't complain. Galveston—The Buccaneer—our furloughs—even Hattiesburg—Dixie Motor Lodge, Petal, Miss Francis, dinner at Holmes, New Orleans, the Edgewater and the magic of the Gulf Coast—and in Galveston, the Balinese Room, Crystal Palace, Nathans, the Martini, the park lunches at the Coast Guard station.

We shall in a sense pay for this beautiful experience for awhile— always longing for each other. But this, like all things, will pass. That is my faith and creed.

All my love and kisses to you. Au revoir for a few days.

Love, Harold

∽

In haste
Sunday, December 9, 1944
(Can't get caught writing this.)

Hello Sweetheart,

At 4 P.M. this afternoon we were suddenly given passes for 12 hours—so, naturally, Sam and I came in.

Actually, I'm not supposed to be writing at all off the post. But I had to write you when, for probably the last time, I can write an uncensored letter.

I just walked down Broadway. It's lonely and I realize how much I miss the big town. I really want to see it with you again.

One more thing—your mail to me will never be censored—write freely but if I ever don't answer anything, don't worry. In a few days there will be another lapse in my writing.

All my love to you all—sit tight—be patient.

And love me, Harold

P.S. I can't tell you the staging area at which I'm located but it's 2 hours from New York City and I won't be here long. Don't repeat anything in this letter.

All my love & kisses, Harold

P.P.S. My morale is high and I feel fine and ready to do my bit to make this country greater—and to protect you. Don't worry—mail will be slow for a couple of weeks—may even stop.

Monday, December 12, 1944

Darling and all,

I'll have to report another day with no mail. Most of the fellows have gotten some, but quite a few of us haven't.

I have been to New York—had dinner at Longchamps at 41st and Broadway with Sam and Walt McGee. Walt is a native Mississippian and I can assure you his eyes really opened. Quite a change from Hattiesburg.

Later we went down to Greenwich Village and I showed the boys the sights. Their eyes really popped at the "Vanguard." Much to my surprise, Sam had never been down there before—as long as he lived in New York.

It was a peculiar feeling, walking down Broadway in uniform. I remember when I was there the first time (I must have been 9 or 10) and we went to a show at the old Globe Theatre and stayed at the Woodstock. And the hundreds of evenings I've spent there since—our trips together—the rainy morning we arrived on our honeymoon. There will never be anything to replace it. The first place we go, darling, when this is over, is to play in little old New York.

I bought two books: *The Sun Is My Undoing* and *The History of Rome*. I'm going to start catching up on my reading. Let's read the same books and compare notes. How about it, sweetheart?

Anxiously awaiting a letter.
With love,
Ever, Harold

ᔪ

December 12, 1944

Dearest,

I just sent a wire to see if everything is OK. I haven't had a letter in a week and want to make sure.

I have been getting re-acquainted on the war effort and, thank God, have recovered my convictions. When we become too deeply involved in a thing as big as this, we are apt to lose our perspective. I was bitter for awhile, because it is the hardest thing in the world for me to imagine living away from you. It is no less hard as time goes on, but I have recovered my faith in what we are doing. Any nation that will not fight for its way of life will not have one for long—we, of all people, should know that. We are only perpetrating a freedom others have fought to give us. That makes us part of a large historical movement going clear back to the Revolution. We should be proud of our part in this greatest of events in our time.

I am not going to feel "away" from you ever. I will always be near you, and whatever I do, I know you'll be there.

Please don't worry. We are taken care of. The government spares no expense in our behalf—above and beyond that, I can take care of myself.

Keep writing and don't be blue. One day this will all be in the past. It is a memory we may not enjoy, but we'll never be ashamed of it.

All my love to you dearest, and to the folks.

Ever, Harold

∽

Wednesday
December 13, 1944

Hello Dearest and all,

I got your wire last night and am glad to know everything is OK.

There certainly is a difference between the location we are now at and Shelby. PX's are wonderful here. Milk is 5 cents a bottle, candy bars, hot dogs—and the places are clean. Shows every night with marvelous talent. It's hard to believe there could be such a difference in camps. These shows that go on are honeys and we have fun among ourselves too. Sam is an invaluable man to have around—he got a big laugh by telling everybody (with a straight face) that we are being transferred to the 741st mess kit repair battalion—in charge of soldering on handles. Morale is surprisingly high and we are prepared to take whatever comes.

I'm still very happy about this outfit. The fellows are really coming thru.

Tonight we're going to another USO variety show.

Give my love to everyone—Flash—mail call and 6 letters for me. Thanks so much. The picture is in my billfold already—send more.

I'm afraid the things I bought you for X-mas will not measure my love for you—but I hope you'll understand I haven't been able to do any real shopping.

You can send my mail AIR MAIL on for 6 cents—all APO mail goes at that price if overseas—up to 1/2 ounce.

Thanks for everything. All my love and kisses to you, sweetheart—I love you with all I've got.

Ever, Harold

P.S. Congrats to Isabelle on the new baby.

P.P.S. Just looked at sales report—wonderful (No. 83, I mean). Trying to show 'em up, huh—you'll have to give most of those girls a handicap. Am re-reading my previous letters. A scarf knitted by you would be a real thrill. I love you so much.

〜

Friday
December 15, 1944

Hello Darling,

Finally I am getting back in my stride—even been reading. I have been interested in the new appointments to the State Department. I must say I am rather disappointed. Mr. Stettinius is a very cultured handsome gentleman, but I'm not convinced he's big enough or liberal enough for the job. Worst of all is Will Clayton—southern plutocrat and industrialist. On the whole, I am keenly disappointed that the President has allowed or perhaps encouraged Stettinius to submit to congress such reactionaries at a time when, soon, our military victories will demand keen and inspired liberalism and faith in democracy in our influence on the rest of the world. Dewey couldn't have done worse. The State Department is as far behind times as it was in Hull's day—and the tragedy is that our victorious Army will be hamstrung by an antiquated diplomatic system. Someone ought to raise a hell of a protest.

I can't get over the food. It is simply marvelous and you get as much as you want.

Everybody here—Joe, Terry, Sam, & the old man send their best to you.

Love and kisses to you, my sweet, and give my best to the folks.

Ever,

Your, Harold

P.S. You will probably get lots of letters like this one when something interests me—I have to share it with you.

⌁

December 17, 1944

Dearest,

There is very little I can tell you in this letter, but I want to keep writing.

We are at sea on a nice ship. We get 2 meals a day. The weather has been pretty good although a few of the boys are seasick (including Sam, boy is he sick). Most of us feel fine. I'm in perfect health. The Red Cross gave us a box each containing a sewing kit, a pack of cards, a package of cigarettes, and some Life-Savers.

We have movies every night.

I hope I'll have some letters when I reach my destination. I know you'll be writing regularly. I won't be writing much but I'll keep them coming.

You know the emptiness I feel in being so far from you but I'll be fine.

All my love, Harold

⌁

December 18, 1944

On Board Ship

Lo Darling,

There is a certain type of excitement in a trip such as we are taking. I can't say I'm disheartened. Of course, I have a gnawing pain in my heart that will never go away until I am once again with you—to stay. But no matter how bad that pain gets—and it will get bad I know—at least will never feel the pain of despair—because I am not only hopeful, I am sure—this is just temporary.

There is a lot of excitement involved in getting into the fight, even though we don't know when or where. It is a peculiar excitement—and everyone seems to be infected with it. It will subside of course and will be replaced by other emotions—God knows what kind.

I have been trying to analyze my own feelings for days (or should I say daze) in regard to finally going over. I really don't know what they are. I've more or less consciously avoided thinking at all. All I know is the time I spend on the other side is going to be rough—plenty rough—especially from the viewpoint of personal feelings. I don't suppose they'll change much from what they now are—loneliness, homesickness, and above all that a great yearning for you, darling. That is my primary emotion.

I wish I could tell you what we are doing, but of course I can't. It is enough to say we are busy and thank God for that. Above all keep writing. It won't do any good for you to ask questions because there is almost nothing I can tell you—and if there is anything I'll tell you.

We all got 3 packs of cigarettes yesterday, a gift accompanied by a letter from President Roosevelt, thanking us for our future efforts.

When I get out of these cramped and crowded quarters where I have time to write without 50 people bothering me all the time, I shall be able to write more coherently.

Meanwhile, I am well and feeling fine—and love you every minute of the day.

Ever, Harold

⌒

Tuesday
December 19, 1944

Hello Darling,

There are now a few things I can tell you. While in the States I was located at Camp Shanks, at Nyack, New York—35 miles up the

Hudson. That was a secret then, but since we've left there for parts unknown, I can tell you. I got into New York just once, for 12 hours, on Sunday a week ago. We were alerted the next day.

You know, I've read so much about going overseas, seen so many movies about it, that I really have to pinch myself to realize I am in the same place today. It's quite a thing—every minute is new and different—in many ways, pleasant and unpleasant—this will be one of the big experiences of my life. And that's the way I'm looking at it—as an experience that I'm going to get as much out of as I can. Not that I wouldn't rather be home—but I'm here and might as well enjoy it while I am able—or at least tolerate it.

By the way, try out both V-Mail and air-mail and I'll let you know which is faster.

I feel that I'm on a stage, playing a part in a big drama. I guess we all are. And don't worry—there are millions of us away and we're coming back sooner than you think.

I don't hear much news, but we learned today the Jerries have launched a counter-offensive east of Aachen. That was inevitable—they'll be pushed back.

Give my best to the folks, and a quick tweak of the nose to you, my dearest.

Ever—
With love, Harold

P.S. I still say goodnight to you every night—and always will.
P.P.S. Sam is still sick as hell, poor guy.

⥿

Wednesday
December 20, 1944

Lo Darling,

Hope you're feeling fine and chipper, as I am now. This is a very pleasant trip—the weather is grand—no storms or anything. Everybody is busy playing cards, reading, or just plain loafing.

Today they had a show on board. It was pretty fair. At least it took up an hour. I have been reading—and not much worthwhile. There isn't much to do but somehow the days go fast.

Sam is still sick. He's really having a miserable time—too bad. Terry and I have been spending some enjoyable hours on deck—we speak of you often—you made quite a hit with him.

Mainly, no matter what I do, I'm thinking of you. It will be a strange holiday season without you. I know it will be hard—for us, but we must make the very best of a temporary situation. I dream of the day I can take you in my arms again—it will be the happiest day of my life. Never fear—and never worry, I love you and I'll come back to you. Please write often and send me more snaps.

All my love, always, Harold

P.S. Just got down to our quarters—some of the boys, led by the indefatigable Lamontagne are whooping out songs accompanied by a guitar. Several political arguments are going on—Lundsgaard and I are still "discussing" the election. Sam is moaning and groaning. He's no sailor. And Phillips (one of the boys you met at Babbitt's house) is going to conduct a Dr. IQ out of a Quiz book—I shall do pretty well.

That's all—goodnight sweetheart, and keep the home fires burning. All my love and devotion,

Harold

Somewhere in England
December 23, 1944

Hello Darling,

As you've noticed from the heading, and the V-Mail Air-Mail note I sent you, I am somewhere in England. That is all we are permitted to say at the present time. I can tell you we had a very nice crossing and everyone arrived in good shape, even Sam Babbitt.

All this is new, so I won't take a chance with censorship yet to tell you anything more. We are eating well, sleeping regularly, and having not too bad a time of it. I haven't been sick a moment and feel tip top.

I was feeling pretty sorry for myself, being so far away from you and home, but I feel differently now. I can't tell you where I am nor what we are doing, but there is one thing about England I can tell you—these people are the grandest people, from the few impressions I've been able to get. They have been in a war for over five years, and believe you me there are no slackers. Everyone knows what war is—just looking at people, you can see that have all suffered much. Not very much like America, and while I thank God we have been spared the real rigors of war on our doorstep, I am sure a lot of people at home would be better off if they could see the guts the people of this island have. No wonder the British rule half the world. It is a real inspiration to me to be with them. There is a lesson in the courage of this people. I guess it is simply the old story of having courage enough to take life as it comes and not feel sorry for ourselves. Simply seeing this has given me a new attitude towards trying to play a man's part. If I know that you are confident and contented with waiting for our future, it will make it much easier for me over here.

Please send me some more pictures of yourself—it's my favorite collector's item. I never knew how much I needed and loved you until you weren't there. There is a gnawing pain in my heart that will always be there until we're together again.

I think you have the harder job. You have to wait until you hear from me. But don't lose heart, I'm with you every minute. I'm anxious to know what you are going to do with your time now that the Christmas rush is over. It's Saturday night and tonight I imagine you'll turn in your book after a busy season. Is it business school, college, or a job in Cleveland?

I'm wearing my heart on my sleeve for you, darling—and always will.

Love and kisses and my best to all the folks and to you a special orchid and all my love for Christmas and the New Year.

All my love, Harold

December 27, 1944
Somewhere in England

Lo Dearest,

Last night I went to town (can't tell you which one, of course) with Sam and we looked the place over. It was very nice—a typical English town, the likes of which you've seen in Dickens and Thackeray. The people are very friendly and I think Sam and I have an invitation to dinner in an English home New Years. The American Red Cross runs a hotel for American troops which is very nice. Food is so scarce that when you are invited to an English home for a meal, the Army provides you with food to take in to compensate for what you eat. Sam and I met these people at a Christmas party for servicemen and local people given at the City Hall last night. I shouldn't have said "Christmas Party"—it was a "Boxing Day Party." The 26th of December in this old and beautiful country is known as Boxing Day. That is the day when the rich or upper classes box presents and take them to the poor—share their Christmas with them, so to speak. It's a very beautiful custom. The Chaplain is writing home here in the office too, tonight, and he said that such a day would be impossible in America, because the poor are, many of them, too proud to accept, and anyway right now the "poor" of other years are riding the crest.

Time out for an argument, friendly of course, with the Chaplain about Mrs. Roosevelt. I, of course, defend her warmly, as usual. I think he's a Republican.

There is a good chance we may get 7-day furloughs in England while we are here. If I get one, I shall try to see as much of this country as possible.

When I observe how much these people have sacrificed for our common cause, I feel very close to the British. You'd like England. When the war is over, we shall have to make a trip here.

I haven't forgotten Dad's birthday on the 1st or Mother's on the 18th. I can't do anything about them, but wish them the happiest of birthdays.

You are the "thing" I'm striving for—to come back to you, my darling—and stay with you forever.

All my love and kisses, Harold

P.S. Please send me 1/2 dozen pair of warm wool sox and a new stainless steel unbreakable mirror.

Ever yours,
Your loving, Harold

P.P.S. I love you, darling, and I miss you like hell.

⌒

Somewhere in England
December 29, 1944

Dearest,

We've seen a good bit of the local countryside in walks. It surely is beautiful and picturesque. Thatched roofs, old stone churches, gabled red brick buildings that look hundreds of years old—all set in a beautiful countryside that seems to come directly out of the "Sketch Book." It is positively charming and seems very homey.

The only thing I need to make my happiness complete is you, darling. Without you, everything is snafu and I live only in hopes for the future. If I had you here I would be having the time of my life—I've always liked the idea of this country even before I saw it. I know that some day when you come over here with me, you will enjoy England and the English people.

I am very anxious to find out how you are and what you're doing. It's been a long time since I've heard from you—home seems far away.

I have been meaning to cable you but up to the present we can't do it. All in all, we have nothing to complain of. We have decent lodgings, good food, and the gang's all here. So don't worry—England is agreeing with me.

Incidentally, the Battery Fund is sponsoring weekly parties—the first was last night—very swell. We had quite a few English guests.

Tonight we had chocolate pudding for supper and cocoa too. It was "My Day."

I told you in the last letter that I've been dreaming of you. The best one was that you came here and told me I had to come home to fix the door knob which was broken. It looks as though the latest German offensive on the other side of the Channel (we don't say overseas anymore) has been stopped. Let's hope it's their last bid.

Well, sweetheart, my heart is full of love and longing for you, darling. I am getting used to being away from you in the sense that I know I must make the best of it, but no one can make me like it. I live only for the day when I can take you in my arms and hug you tight. When that day comes I shall be the happiest man in the world and I'll make you the happiest woman.

> Ever and always—
> Faithfully yours, Harold

Somewhere in England
December 30, 1944

Sweetheart Darling,

It's Saturday night and most of the boys have gone to town, but I feel like sitting here and talking to you.

I have never told you about this place, so here goes. We live in temporary type barracks heated by coal stoves. Each barracks has 5 rooms—a large non-com's room and four smaller rooms for other enlisted men. We have running water and a shower but seldom have hot water. We have electric lights. There is no longer a blackout even in military areas in England. Our "mattresses" are straw ticks like they use in Boy Scout camps. Not too comfortable but we are learning to sleep on them.

The food is sometimes very good, sometimes awful. But on the whole it's OK—better than you can buy in an English restaurant.

We have a P.X. but buying is strictly rationed. For example, once a week you can buy 5 packs of cigarettes, 4 bars of candy, 3 packages of cookies, 2 boxes of matches, I cake of soap, 2 packs of gum. Every 2 weeks you can buy 4 ounces of peanuts, 1 cake of laundry soap, 1 package of razor blades. Every 4 weeks a tube of tooth paste, one of shaving cream, a writing kit, and pipe cleaners. Every 8 weeks a tooth-brush, 1 pack of cards, 1 comb, 2 flashlight batteries, 1 can lighter fluid, 1 bottle ink, 1 jar Nescafe (Yep!), 1 pipe, 1 face towel, 1 bath towel. I quote all this to show you how we live when war is going on. Civilians get far less of these things. We each have a ration card. If you lose it it's TS until a new one is issued. It's adequate but not exactly super-abundant.

We have movies 3 nights a week and USO shows occasionally. The people in town (sorry I still can't tell you what town) are very hospitable and passes are plentiful.

I know it would be more interesting if I could tell you names and dates—but I can't. We play cards, read, wash our clothes (that Lux washability expert should see me washing wool underwear) and work. We follow the news avidly, naturally enough—it looks plenty good right now.

My main desire is word from home. I know a pile of it is accumulating en route and I'll take a day off to read it.

Keep your chin up, dear. This half of the partnership is pretty confident and therefore reasonably content. A very good New Year to the folks—and when the bells ring out this year—I'll be with you at home—God bless you.

Ever,
Your, Harold

Somewhere in England
January 7, 1945

Sweetheart Darling,

Two months to the day since I got you folks off to Wooster—one month since we headed for P.O.E. and last night I got 3 letters so it has been my biggest day since hitting England. Our NCO radio is playing here in the hut on this snowy Sunday afternoon—"Swing and Sway" with Sammy Kaye. So, with word from you finally, I am as much at peace with the world as I expect to ever be until I can have you in person.

You're very welcome to the $35 a month. With the insurance, family allotment, and bond also deducted I have about 4 pounds (4£ = $16.00) a month left which is plenty.

I gather from your letters (which I've read and reread a dozen times each) that the winter is pretty severe at home. Today's snow is our first—it's cozy to sit here and watch it.

The war news on the front looks better the last three days. If "Jerry" can't break out of the Ardennes or prosecute his advantage further south at the Vosges within a very short time he'll never be able to do it. But there is fight left in him yet—contrary to our optimistic hopes.

I imagine it was hard for you to wait until you found out what theatre I was in.

I knew you'd go to the family party at Oakwood—I was there on Christmas Day in spirit.

I'm praying too the war is over soon—every day. I'm pretending I'm with you, sweet, and living for the day when it will be so.

All my love to you, and don't worry—Uncle Sammy is taking good care of me.

Ever yours with all my heart,

Harold

Somewhere in England
January 10, 1945

Darling,

I've been very lucky with my mail; today I got your first V-Mail written December 30th.

One of our principal activities here is washing our own clothes. Let me tell you I don't like it one bit, and no matter how often I do it I won't get used to it. Sergeant Lassiter has just bought an electric iron and some of the boys are washing their ODs. We can get one week cleaning service. I did try washing one of those Palm Beach ties. It looks like hell, but I'll iron it and see how it comes out. Oh, I'll be a handy little housewife for you when I get out of here.

The food is holding up pretty well, but I could use a box of goodies with a few pair of thick wool sox thrown in. Thanks.

Today is nice and sunny after several dark snowy ones. I've managed to stay clear of all but an occasional sniffles—feel pretty good.

The gang sends their best to you—Terry says to tell you hello especially—told me he thinks you're a swell gal. Joe wants me to send you a kiss—I'd like to deliver that in person.

Send my regards to the gang in Galveston. Just a year ago we were getting ready to leave there—the fifth of February wasn't it? I still want to go back in civvies.

My love to everyone—especially the folks and Donald—and your mail is coming thru, keep up the good work sweetie.

Ever and always,
With love, Harold

Somewhere in England
January 16, 1945

Sweetheart,

I see by the *Stars and Stripes* that the Cleveland Electric Company
has been taken over by the government after a disgraceful strike.
Having been so proud of Ohio's war record, Yates, Uffner, and I are
taking quite a beating from the boys for this strike—at a time when
every nerve is being strained over here. What in the hell is the matter
with those people anyhow? I don't want to be unreasonable, but from
this distance it certainly stinks. Other news from home that sounds
interesting is that you girls will be wearing more abbreviated clothing
this summer. That is a release straight from the garment district
according to *Stars & Stripes*. I don't see how they could be more abbreviated than some of the local yokels wore last summer.

The Daily Records up to the 16th of December came today—a
whole flock of them. Freedlander's ad looked good this Christmas. I
didn't see much in the personals that interested me. I did notice where
Ken Rhode got a promotion in the Navy.

I haven't told you about the English money. We are quite adept at it
now, not having had American money since we got here. The English
have a penny (pence they call it) which is worth 1-2/3 cents American
money. Twelve pence makes a shilling (20 cents), twenty shillings make
a pound ($4.00). The actual coins are a half-penny (pronounced by
our British friends something like aypenny); a penny; a three-pence
(pronounced thrupence) which is worth an American nickel; a sixpence (worth a dime); a shilling (20 cents). Above the basic shilling is
a florin (2 shilling piece); a half-crown (2 1/2 shillings—50 cents); a
crown (5 shillings—$1.00 and rarely used); a ten shilling note ($2.00
bill); and the pound note. There are undoubtedly larger bills. The half-
penny is copper colored and about the size of a quarter. The penny
same color, the size of a half dollar. The three-pence is hexagonal in
shape and a shinier copper. The sixpence is almost a dead ringer for a

dime (which is exactly what it's worth). The shilling is silver and the size of a quarter. The florin is between a quarter and half dollar in size and also silver. The half-crown is same size, color, and weight almost as the half dollar. The crown is gold and they are struck off only on great occasions such as a coronation, birth of an heir presumptive to the throne, or the marriage of one of the immediate royal family. The ten shilling note is much wider than our dollar bill but about the same length. The pound note is same width but a little longer. And that is your lesson. It sounds funny at our blackjack and rummy games to hear Babbitt, Joe, or myself say, "raise you one and three" (1 shilling, three-pence—25 cents). English cigarettes are lousy and very expensive—they cost 2 and 3 for 20. Guess how much? Exactly! 45 cents. At the Red Cross we get meals for 1 and 3 and pay 2 shillings for a bed for the night. A movie may cost you anywhere from 1 and 3 to 2 and 9 (25 cents to 55 cents) depending upon where you sit. The best seats are the front of the balcony (called the upper circle over here), next is the rear of the balcony, then the rear of the main floor (orchestra seats are referred to as stalls), and last the cheapest seats are the front of the stall section.

One night last week Sam, Terry, and I went into town (still can't tell you which one), and there was a dance at the Red Cross so we stopped by. It amazed me the way these English girls jitterbug. They are real fanatics about it—I saw fellows who couldn't do it left right in the middle of the floor. They're catching on fast.

I imagine this will reach you between our anniversary and your birthday. Darling, you know that I am thinking what you are thinking now because when people are happy together, anniversaries and birthdays too don't call for an artificial outpouring. I won't love you a bit more on those days than I do today or will twenty years from now—or fifty if we're still here. But I'll love you as much as I can possibly love anyone. I won't wish you happy anniversary and birthday because they aren't happy. I send you my fondest love and the old story that you will be my beloved forever. This temporary separation will be over and will fade into the past—but you will always be the bride I held in my arms the 23rd of January 1939. And your birthdays to me are just an excuse to show you how much you mean to me. I'm as hopelessly in love as I was six years ago and will be forever.

I love you my darling, for all of life,

Harold

〜

January 21, 1945
Sunday

Dearest,

About two hours ago your cable arrived. Thank you, sweetheart. It meant a lot.

The BBC has been telling us all day the Russians are 100 miles west of Warsaw. There is no sign of a let up yet, and I don't think they intend to stop. I hope Berlin is their next goal. The fighting on Luzon is going well too. When Tarlac falls, it should be about half over there—and now our troops in the Ardennes have reached St. Vith, which will write off Rundstedt's gamble as a failure.

The English I've talked to seem very optimistic. They think it will be over during spring. I'll admit it doesn't seem impossible anymore.

Everybody here is talking about Mrs. Elliott Roosevelt's dog who got priority over two or three servicemen on a transcontinental plane. Somebody slipped badly there. That was a hell of a note.

The radio is pretty good today. We just heard Sammy Kaye's *Swing and Sway* music. Also—there is a Gilbert & Sullivan on the air shortly. When I go to London I'd like to go to Covent Garden to see one.

Happy anniversary, dearest, and all my love to you, on this lonesome anniversary. We'll just skip this one.

Love & kisses, Harold

〜

Somewhere in England
January 21, 1945

Darling,

I figure you will get this letter about the time that a year ago we left Texas. A lot has happened in the last year, hasn't it? I never would have believed that we would have so much of it together when that train pulled out of Camp Wallace on February 5th. I have sort of been reviewing the year in my mind. The black feeling I had when I first saw Camp Shelby—the 69th division—"Bolte's Bivouackin' Bastards"—out in the field all the time—the break Mr. Luquette gave me when he got me on the cadre of the 219th. Then that furlough home, the trip back to Mississippi we three made, weekends at Biloxi and Gulfport, our four "homes" in Hattiesburg—the Saenger, Homes's, K.C. Steak House, Jules Landrys—New Orleans and the Monteleone, Roosevelt, Pat O'Brien's and the mint juleps that made you tight on a bright Sunday afternoon (yes you were, too). Our friends in Hattiesburg—Vivian and Leo, Nat and Sam, Shirley and Sy. Oh yes, and Miss Francis and her mother and the kids. Our gulf—our whole Army career in the States is based on it. Anyhow, these "foolish things remind me of you"—in spite of the greasy food, the waiting in line, the heat, and the general living conditions. It was an experience we could share together and enjoy. It made us aware that it is not physical things that count in real happiness. I shall never be afraid of poverty. I know we, together, can do without anything but each other.

At first I thought such reminiscing would be bad for me, but it seems to have the effect of pepping me up. Somehow, when I think of all we have together, I feel more confident of the future.

Your cable made me realize how close we are. As long as we both remember and treasure the days, that is what counts.

I see the U.S. is having a brown-out now. I suppose all lights in store windows go out at dusk and stay out all night. At the rate business has been going I'm sure they won't miss the extra business.

Tomorrow is usually a big mail day. I'm looking forward to it. Mail is one thing you can't get too much of around here.

The food we get isn't too bad. We get plenty of powdered eggs, but it all depends on what cook prepares them. If he's careless they are lousy, if not, they taste fairly good. Tonight we had chicken. We eat ten times better than the British civilians. I'm really sorry for them.

Well, dear, I hope everyone is well at home and that you're keeping your chin up. My love to the folks, both in Wooster and Cleveland. I shall continue to mail to Wooster since your cable sent the 18th came from there.

All my love, Harold

ᔪ

January 26, 1945

Darling,

I have just returned from a 3-day pass (we are not allowed to send mail on pass). I spent this one in the Midlands Center of Birmingham. It is one of England's largest cities and probably comparable in industry to Detroit.

One thing very obvious there is the effect of the Blitz. The Huns didn't neglect Birmingham and there are piles of rubble and shells of buildings all over the city.

I went to the Red Cross and joined a party taking a tour. We saw the Cathedral (they're all gorgeous and all alike), the college, the various memorials, and a tremendous amount of industry. Incidentally, the Timken Roller Bearing Co. Ltd. is located in Birmingham. On the front of the building it says: Canton, Mount Vernon, Wooster, Columbus, Ohio, USA; Birmingham, England; Stockholm, Sweden; Paris, France. Was I proud of that. I also met a couple of fellows at the Red Cross and we went to a review, *Alice in Wonderland*. It was a London company and they had made an adult musical comedy out of the thing. Pretty fair.

Thursday something unusual happened. I was having brunch in a coffee shop on Coleman Row in Victoria Square and a middle-aged gentleman sitting opposite started talking to me. He said he'd been often to America and asked me where I was from. When I said Ohio he almost fell out of his chair. He is married to a "girl" from Cleveland, brought her over here some 30 years ago. Well to make a long story shorter, I was taken to his home for dinner. His wife, a charming lady, was overwhelmed. I stayed so late I nearly missed the last train back to town. They were really wonderful. He had to tell me that I had done his wife more good than he could say. He was very nice and she was so grateful just to talk to someone from home. I guess you never forget where your roots are.

Today it snowed plenty hard and I had to forego my pilgrimage to Stratford-on-Avon to see Shakespeare's home because the busses didn't run. That is all I shall go back to the Midlands for.

We're getting cold weather now—snowed—most every day. My cold is 100% better. The Red Army is saving us a lot of trouble. And General MacArthur is only 40 miles from Manila.

More tomorrow, darling, and tell Mom I'll write her soon.

All my love & kisses to you, sweetheart.

Yours Ever, Harold

Somewhere in England
January 29, 1945

Darling,

This is the ninth day since I've had mail.

Well, the Russians march on! I haven't heard a report tonight yet, but I believe the Reds are about 80 miles from Hell (Berlin) at last report. I hope they beat us there and turn the Cossacks loose on the whole damned civilian population. I suppose the sob-sisters and "good" church people are starting to tsk tsk about a hard peace. If they do, they ought to pick them out of their prayer meetings and send 'em over here to see what the Germans have done. The only good Kraut is a dead one. There are getting to be a lot of good ones, and that's something to ring the church bells about.

How's everything at home? By the time you get this, I shall no doubt have plenty of news from you and believe me I'm anxious to get it.

I still (and always shall) say goodnight to you each night, dearest. I hope you're coming thru this awful winter OK. Take good care of yourself.

I can't begin to tell you how I long for you. I know the meaning now of the song—"The Very Thought of You."

Goodnight, sweetheart, till we talk tomorrow.

Harold

Somewhere in England
January 29, 1945

Dear Mother & Dad,

Thanks so much for your telegram on our anniversary. I was so tickled to find it when I returned from Birmingham.

I had a chance to talk to a good many English soldiers while in Birmingham and I was surprised at the way they felt about the differences between our two countries. Most of the British admit this country is 50 years behind America. They say social and political reforms have been instituted here during the war (such as the Beveridge Plan, which they call Blitz Benevolence) but they insist that victory will find the old ruling classes in the saddle as firmly as ever and that a lot of the reforms will die out because of indirect opposition. The masses are used to staying put, and the classes will rule again, they say. After all, while this is a liberal monarchy, it is a monarchy. I was amazed at how many young English feel this way and hope to emigrate to the Dominions after victory. Canada is most popular, followed by Australia, New Zealand, and South Africa. Very few want to go to the

U.S. I don't know if many will do it or if I even got a cross-section of opinion, but those are my impressions. It is interesting to see how honest these people are about the country they have fought so hard to preserve.

The Red Army is still sweeping on. We are hoping our boys will be able to shake hands with the "Comrades" soon.

I hope you are all well and feel cheerful. I've been tremendously pepped up by the military developments of the past two weeks. Perhaps it won't be too long until I can put my feet under your table again, Mom. Speed the day.

Love and kisses, Harold

↬

Somewhere in England
February 11, 1945

Dearest,

I am back from London safe and sound. It's hard to try to put experiences of four days "rubbernecking" on paper.

First of all I looked up Geoffrey and Claire's parents, the Greenbury's, at the S. Weiss store on Shaftesbury Street. They are perfectly charming people. We had lunch together. Their original store was about the size of ours but has been bombed out. Geoffrey was sent directly to France some months ago and, close as he is, they don't have any idea how long it will be before they see him.

I hardly know how to begin. I went with Bob Lassiter. The first thing we did was take a tour of the city arranged for visiting G.I.s by the Red Cross. We saw St. James Palace, Buckingham Palace, the Houses of Parliament, Thames Embankment, the Strand (chief shopping district), the Tower of London (not really a tower at all but a prison where much of the bloody history of the Stuart and Tudor kings and queens took place), Westminster Abbey (the burial ground of the Empire's great—statesmen, poets, kings, philosophers), and St. Paul's Cathedral which still stands among a bombed area. We saw

Whitehall (the street where the government buildings stand), the War Ministry, the Foreign Office, the Law Courts, No. 10 Downing Street (but Winny wasn't standing in front—you know No. 10 is the house of the Prime Minister), Dickens Old Curiosity Shop, and the great centers of traffic known all over the world—Leicester Square, Trafalgar Square, Picadilly Circus (Circus is just a round square), and Oxford Circus.

That finished up day number one. The next day, I went down to Buckingham Palace to see the changing of the guard, but it was post-poned and I missed it. They only have it a few times a month in wartime.

In the evening I went to Covent Garden—the Royal Opera House—where I expected to see a show but found a huge dance going on. It is a gorgeous place—something like the Met in New York. We watched the dancing and I danced with some ATS girls (British WACS). The third morning I went to the British Museum. Most of the valuable things have been removed, but there was still plenty for a one-time history major to see. That afternoon I saw the British come-dy hit of the season with Sid Field, a Cockney Jewish comedian. It was terribly funny—particularly the Paris and golfing scenes.

That night I wandered around the downtown district around Picadilly and Leicester Square with Bob.

The last day I visited the Tower of London—which is one of the great monuments to London's bloody past. Elizabeth, Mary Queen of Scots, Essex, Raleigh, and thousands of others (including Queen Anne Boleyn and two other unfortunate wives of Henry VIII) were "guests" here. Most of them left it headless. It was a real revival of my English history. My last little excursion was a walk across London Bridge, which has been falling down for 500 years. These Tower guides are dressed in medieval costume.

Notes: The Underground (subway) is marvelous—something like the new 8th Avenue line only much deeper.

It's a wonderful city and the famous places are just like you would expect them to be—it is a seat of empire and power. There is only one London just like there is only one New York. We'll see it together sometime. On Whitehall you can almost feel the power that keeps this old Empire rolling along, however erratically.

By the way—at Covent Garden there was a Russian delegation and they stopped the dancing to play "Meadowland" and then proceeded the playing of "God Save the King" with the new Soviet Anthem.

But all the time, dearest, I kept thinking it would be perfect if I only had you along to enjoy it too.

I love you—always—adorable.

Your, Harold

⌒

Somewhere in England
February 14, 1945

Lo Darling,

Until tonight I hadn't burned a single letter of yours or Mother's, so I had a bonfire—burned all but the most recent. You've been wonderful about writing and I know you'll keep it up, sweetheart. Your mail to me is the mostest thing I could want over here.

I was very interested in hearing that you are going back to Wooster the first of March. Of course you must spend some time with Mother and Dad in Cleveland. They've been perfectly swell about everything. As you say, Wooster is going to be our home, and it will be nice if you feel like it's home when I get back. And Mother idolizes you. You mean so much to her—you really have no idea. I'm not exaggerating when I say that you are as dear to her as Dad or myself. She will get by all right if you can be with her—but I'm not going to tell you what to do.

From your letters, I am very happy that your morale is high. Keep it there, baby—it does me a world of good to know you are as cheerful as possible. No matter how impatient you may get, just keep your chin up. And continue to keep me informed on everything that goes on at home.

That's all for tonight. By the way, please send me some cotton shirts and shorts and a pocket knife. Thanks, dearest.

All my love to the folks, and a big hug and kiss for my one and only sweetheart. I love you so much.

Your, Harold

~

Somewhere in England
February 19, 1945

Lo Darling,

Today I did something I didn't think I would have to do—cabled you for money. I have been on about $17.25 a month for two months which I thought would be plenty, but we have had so much more opportunity for passes and to go into town for dinners, shows, and to sleep off post than I thought that I've been running low. I've already borrowed a couple of pounds and shall probably have to borrow at least another. I wanted to tell you why I asked for it so you don't wonder whether I'm gambling it away.

We are now authorized to wear a theatre ribbon. Now I have two Good Conducts and the ETO ribbon. If I stay long enough I'll look like a Christmas tree.

The radio is making me terribly homesick for 818, our piano, the living room, den, and everything that means just you. They just played "These Foolish Things Remind me of You"—and they do. Also "Music Maestro Please" which brings up memories of the days when I was courting you.

Getting back to the radio again, we hear all the old familiars that were part of our life, and I have my happiest moments in reminiscence—I loved our doll house. The two years we spent wandering the country are slipping away from me already. Civilian days are the ones I am really looking forward to—when no longer will Army orders ever separate us. In short, I am building my dream castles that belong to you and me.

Give my regards to the folks, stay the same as you always have been, and I'll always love you darling.

G'nite, Harold

↜

Somewhere in England
February 22, 1945

Lo Darling,

Frankie Sinatra is on the air and so the mood is appropriately romantic.

The longer I am over here, the more I challenge myself as to the real cause of this war, and the relationship you and I have. I have wondered whether I might become cynical after suffering this separation which must of necessity drag out. I've wondered whether I could keep my ideals which include my own participation in this war along with my craving for you. At times I have felt that I might lose the ideals. I have also kept up my interest in what goes on in the world and that includes more than just war news. I've been following the fight in regard to the Wallace appointment. I am interested in seeing that men with the fine principles and courage of Henry Wallace stay in the government.

The main thing you have to do is to be a man and keep your sense of humor. Too many fellows have the feeling that they have been terribly imposed upon. Perhaps they have. We all have. It isn't a pleasant thing to leave your family and particularly a wife to whom you're devoted and live a soldier's life thousands of miles from home. I have tried to keep in mind that this is a very personal war. The things we believe in we'll still have to fight for, and for the kind of world we want to live in. But if our enemies were winning this war instead of losing it, we wouldn't last long and if we did life would be unbearable. We are defending our way of life by destroying them. And while that may not sound very idealistic, it is fact.

While feeling that way has made me feel a lot better, nothing will make me really content. You know what I mean because you feel the same way. We're just marking time while waiting to have each other again. That's a hard thing to go thru day after day—probably much harder for you than for me. Nothing is worse than this interminable waiting and it's only been a little over 3-1/2 months since we saw each other.

Radio Berlin is on with her propaganda program beamed to England. Always good for a laugh, so I shall listen.

All my love to you, sweetheart,

Harold

⌒

Somewhere in England
February 26, 1945

Lo Sweet,

This letter will be for you and the folks too.

Your packages and Mother's have been swell—the canned stuff is what we want.

Your telling about Helen Weil's graduation brought me back to that day you were graduated. I was so much in love then that all I could do was look at you and think of you. Not until I married you and had you with me constantly did I realize how lucky I am. I am more than ever in love now. I was used to a good home before I was married, and I guess I was spoiled a little. Well, you completed the process. My home life, which has been in your hands ever since January 23, 1939, has been nothing but a joy. I say all this because, I think, it does me good once in awhile to let you know, and Mother and Dad too, how much I appreciate what I think is the finest thing a man can have—a grand Mom and Pop and a wife you can love, adore, and admire. I have all of that for which I thank God.

I get sentimental occasionally but I always feel this in my heart. My fondest hope and future dream is to come back to you soon and stay with you forever. Everything else is secondary. This business I'm in now teaches real values.

My best to you all, and take care of yourselves. A big hug and a long kiss, beloved.

With my everything,
Your, Harold

⌒

Somewhere in England
March 2, 1945

Dearest Lo,

The news is surely good right now. Our gains on the 9th, 1st, and 3rd Army fronts may not look impressive in territory gained compared to the Red drives of last month, but we are not trying to gain ground so much as we are destroying the Wehrmacht. We are getting pretty close to the Rhine—6 miles from Cologne at last report. I have a bet with Les Myers that the organized German resistance with the Nazi Party ruling Germany will be over May 1st at the latest. I think I'll win.

I was very satisfied with the results of the Yalta Conference. Of course we shall have to wait for the San Francisco Conference in order to really tell what's happening. Our delegation is very encouraging. I'm glad to see Dean Virginia Gildersleeve of Barnard on the delegation. She is one of the outstanding American women of our age in my opinion. I have set great hopes by this conference just because I believe a preliminary organization must be set up before we, of the United Nations, drift apart when the pressure of war is off. To let the purpose of a world peace organization with teeth in it die at this time will be race suicide for the generation now being born. As Americans we must be prepared to sacrifice some of our own sovereignty in order that we can live in a decent world. It should be an interesting post-war world to watch.

Requests: more stationery, more pictures, and some melba toast and liver paste.

I love you very much, my beloved.

> Ever,
> Your, Harold

᠁

> Somewhere in France
> March 8, 1945

Lo Darling & Folks,

So this is France! As you know, I can't tell you what part I'm in. I can tell you the people here carry in their eyes the effect of 4 years under the Nazis. They are very poorly dressed for the most part and the kids look hungry. They are all very polite and exceedingly friendly. But you get the feeling you are witnessing people who have something horrible to live down. Most of the men are very old or very young. Their wages are poor and all are suffering from the fluctuations of the franc. Not much like the light-hearted people I remember 15 years ago. Damn the Germans!

The war news is certainly wonderful? First Cologne, and soon Coblenz and Bonn. Remember, I told you we were due to break loose? And I think the Russians are on the verge of the crash there.

I must tell you, as ever, adorable, that I say goodnight every night to the sweetest girl in the world—God how I love you.

My love to all of you and please keep writing.

To you, darling, a fond kiss.

> Love & kisses, Harold

᠁

A young, well-dressed Harold Freedlander

Harold and Lois Freedlander saying goodbye at
the train station in Wooster

Basic Training • Galveston, Texas 1943
Harold Freedlander—standing second from the right

Corporal Freedlander
Galveston, Texas

Harold & Lois Freedlander with good friends Natalie & Sam Babbitt
Hattiesburg, Mississippi

Harold & Lois
Freedlander at
Camp Wallace
Galveston, Texas

Harold Freedlander
at his desk
at the Anti-Aircraft Division

Bernie Snyder, Ray Bowman and Harold Freedlander
with the jeep "Charlona" at the front with the Ninth Army • May 1945

Harold Freedlander in front of the Baron Von Wildhausen estate
Gersfeld Germany • Labor Day 1945

Harold Freedlander at his desk
Darmstadt Germany • November 1945

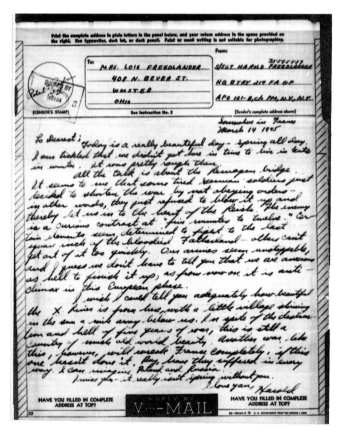

A sample of V-Mail

Staff Sergeant Freedlander with an anti-aircraft gun
Detmold, Germany • 1945

Harold Freedlander with friend Terry Ryan Melsungen, Germany • 1945

Staff Sergeant Freedlander and friends with captured Nazi flag

"Old Glory" over Deutchland • 1945

Christa and Gretchen—German children— with Sergeant Freedlander
in Gersfeld, Germany • September 22, 1945

Bernie Snyder and Harold Freedlander
with two Buchenwald survivors—
"the thrill of their sad, tragic lives"

Harold Freedlander holding Siegfried
Darmstadt, Germany • October 25, 1945

HAROLD H. FREEDLANDER

To you who answered the call of your country and served in its Armed Forces to bring about the total defeat of the enemy, I extend the heartfelt thanks of a grateful Nation. As one of the Nation's finest, you undertook the most severe task one can be called upon to perform. Because you demonstrated the fortitude, resourcefulness and calm judgment necessary to carry out that task, we now look to you for leadership and example in further exalting our country in peace.

Harry Truman

Harold Freedlander delivering Commencement Address
Wooster High School • May 30, 1982

Somewhere in France
March 8, 1945

Dearest Lo and Folks,

B.B.C. from London has just announced that word was received a half hour ago (7:30 P.M.) that our troops have crossed the Rhine and established a bridge head. What wonderful news! I really can't see how it can be much longer. And the bombing of Berlin has really been savage, but no more than they deserve.

When the San Francisco Conference is held next month please send me the best clippings you can find. We get all the essentials of the news, but I miss the commentary. I'm asking now so that you can collect them. That sort of thing will still be timely when I get it. I believe it will be awfully important for us all.

The radio has been playing some wonderful old songs we love— such as "Imagination" (which I use constantly to bring you close), "Music Maestro Please," "These Foolish Things." I just lay back on my bed and closed my eyes and was with you again. In fact I am really home every day. I can see every detail of the life I love in my mind's eye. The bridge games with Mom & Pop, hamburgers at the Liberty, the evening trips to the store where we had so much fun (trying on hats for instance), and all the things we did and will do again. Maybe we're just kids and will always act like kids, but what do we care—we'll always be happy. Just stay as you are.

So for now, goodnite.

I love you, always,
Harold

My Dearest,

Another day and what news we have had today—the Rhine crossed, Goebbels home turned over to Jewish soldiers for a synagogue, our armies on the march to the Swiss frontier, the Russians 28 miles from Berlin. Some events—and the Reich crumbling visibly.

It's awfully hard to write since there's so little that we can say. Today I had my first shower in a week—boy will I appreciate a daily shower when I return home.

We live in tents and have cots and while life is very simple it is adequate. Joe gives us good chow and no one is going hungry.

To get back to the French people, I have noticed that those who have a few clothes to wear have a lot more style than British women, and prettier legs too. No, dear, don't worry, I'm just looking them over but when it comes to anything else, you are the only gal for me—I'm more convinced of that every minute we're apart.

By the way, more pictures, please.

Don't worry about me. I eat regularly, sleep regularly, and everything is OK. At the rate this war is going, I can't see how the Huns can avoid destruction if this keeps up much longer.

My love to you all—and thank God every night you live in the U.S.A., for you are spared all these people went thru. We're here to see you will always be spared it.

Love, Harold

Somewhere in France
March 10, 1945

Lo Dearest,

This was a frosty morning. When I crawled out of my ducky little sleeping bag and hit the deck I thought I would turn to a block of ice. Spring, where art thou? After moving around a bit and having my grapefruit juice, hot cakes, and coffee I was warmed up. It's almost noon now and it's going to be a beautiful day.

Did the store have a Dollar Day this year? I suppose not. I find I'm missing the store quite a bit, far more than I did while in the States. Just part of natural homesickness.

It would be impossible to realize until you go thru it just how much you want a normal life. I used to think I wanted a lot of travel and excitement, but darling, I am going to be able to find all I want in a radius of a few hundred miles from home—just enough to include New York. Anywhere you are is home for me—even Hattiesburg. Speaking of Hattiesburg, yesterday was a good day for memories among the old vets of the outfit since it was March 9 a year ago that the 219th was activated at Shelby. Still left of the original 20 of us are Sam, Lassiter, Snyder, Price, Grimaldi, as well as about 8 others—about 14 of us from the original cadre out of the 69th. As long as I have to wear olive drab this outfit is my home in the Army—although God knows I'm over-ready for a return to normal living. This life is only an existence—not life.

I hope you're feeling OK and that you are keeping your chin up. Be patient.

I love you, dearest.
Ever,
your, Harold

⟿

My Darling,

This is a beautiful spring day at last—brilliant sunshine and a timid attempt in the middle of the day for warm weather.

Isn't the news wonderful? Austria has just fallen to the Russians and the 1st Army is taking full advantage of the lucky break at the Ludendorff Bridge. There is probably plenty of fighting ahead which seems a pity since the result is now so certain. But whatever it takes, our allies and ourselves have the stuff to see it thru.

How is everything on the home front? I'm so anxious for news from you, dear. The biggest contribution I am able to make for my own peace of mind will be patience—I say "will" because it's pretty hard to wait for the end of the rainbow when the pot of gold holds such a delectable treasure as you, darling.

I went down for a shower today. The round trip to the showers takes a couple of hours. A couple a week is all you ever get time for, but I really feel like a new person.

They say we'll have more mail tomorrow. The best moments are when I can be with you.

Ever, and adoringly,
Your, Harold

⌒

Somewhere in France
March 15, 1945

Lo Dearest,

I had an opportunity of visiting a town last evening and Johnny Hiza and I smacked our lips over some pretty good cognac. France's pride and joy—fine wines and liquors—has suffered a lot, but they still have some pretty good stuff in the cafes. A glass of cognac costs 20 francs at least (40¢). It isn't a cheap indulgence. I really have no great liking for liquor, but I shall probably continue to visit the cafes once in a while, mainly for the purpose of getting away from Army routine for a couple of hours. France is so short of food that it is a court martial offense to buy or eat food purchased from a civilian source—so restaurant visiting is out and you eat in the mess line or not at all! For the most part our food is far superior to what they have to eat over here.

Surprisingly enough, many Frenchmen were getting used to the German occupation, and while not exactly Nazis, resented our coming. Whenever a complete change of regime comes about some people benefit by it and resent any interference. France was a sort of model occupation like Denmark, and since most Frenchmen are realistic and philosophical, they learned to accept it. The Germans were very strict in suppressing the black market here and now that the French government is in power again, corruption has increased, thereby making goods scarcer and practically impossible for the poorer classes to buy. I was talking to the Colonel about this last evening, and it is his opinion that had the Germans continued to occupy France up to a total of 10 years they would probably have won. I don't mean we are not welcome—most Frenchmen probably feel we have helped to start them on the road back, but you do get a lot of blank looks. I personally think it is due to the current food shortage and the allied bombings necessary to drive the Germans out. Whatever it is, it rather surprises me. Compared to the friendly English, France is polite but cold. The British troops find it even more so. In the long run I'm sure old hurts will be forgotten and I'm not going to be too sensitive to the sometimes puzzling attitude of a half-starved, war-ravaged people. This republic has in the past too fine a record to be sold out quickly now.

My French is picking up slowly but surely—j'ai pensé que j'ai perdu la touche mais il me viens. If I were to spend enough time here I'd pick it up quickly because I like the language.

I'll sign off while listening to the Harry James band. Our programs from home are tops.

The news continues good.

All my love to you, my darling, and keep your pretty little chin up.

Ever,

Your, Harold

⇜

March 20, 1945

My Darling,

We are somewhere in Germany. That is all I can tell you geographically. But I can assure you we are safer than most of the people crossing the street at Euclid and 9th.

Over here we don't live in the field. The procedure is this: when an outfit moves into an area in Germany, civilian houses are picked for them and the residents are told to leave—the American Military Government provides other quarters for them. So we are living in a lovely home—with easy chairs, couches, linoleum, and bathrooms. I sleep on a beautiful soft mattressed big double bed. I never had it so good. I can imagine what the Germans think of all this but they are not the super race any more. As one officer put it—Americans will not sleep in the fields while Germans live indoors. So we have an almost unbelievable setup here.

I will continue to tell you as much as I may. I know you want to know a lot more, but please remember I'll do all I can to keep you informed. There is nothing to worry about—I'm eating swell and sleeping like a log. Back home "Germany" probably sounds terrible but remember that occupied Germany is also where the American flag flies.

I have visited Belgium and Holland and also Aachen—and all you've heard about the latter is true ten times over. What a job— Germany can never forget this.

Incidentally—we are not allowed to speak to, smile at, or fraternize in any way with any German man, woman, or child. No candy for the kids—we just look right thru them. The Army looks on all of them as Nazis—but to see the white flags out on houses that probably flew the swastika before is a very heartening sight—and they all say they hate Hitler. Oh yeah?

> With all my love—
> Ever—
> Your, Harold

꿈

> Somewhere in Germany
> March 21, 1945

Lo Dearest,

Terry and I have been sitting in our pleasant German living room on a couple of easy chairs discussing business—our real business. Terry's been telling me some of his experiences in the furniture mart in Chicago, and I have been recalling my many episodes in the good old New York market. It's a good thing that I have one person around here that talks my language—it's almost like home.

In spite of the fact that we're in Germany, living so comfortably like this in a home makes me feel very close to home. I am more than ever anxious to be with you again, sharing the daily experiences. I can't help but feel that that moment is not too far away—and I will admit that I pray for it to come soon. The longer I have to do without you the less patience I have.

> I love you, sweetheart.
> Ever,
> Your, Harold

꿈

Lo Darling,

It's 74 months today since we said "I do" at the Wade Park Manor. Today is just the same kind of day, too. Warm, sunshiny, balmy—those first days of spring have always reminded me of our first spring together—the experience of our own little home, the easy change we both made to married life, and the delight of having you to come home to every night. That has never changed for me—you're still my bride, darling. It's longer from the time I said goodbye in November until the happy day when I'll say hello—I know that the same sweet girl will be waiting for me. I often think back to those evenings in our den when the terrible news came in—from Poland, Belgium, France, Russia, the Balkans and the Pacific. It all seemed so dark then—and here we are in Germany, not as slaves or POWs, but as a victorious conquering army along with our allies who have fought so long and so bravely. No, I wouldn't be elsewhere. I have hated Fascism for as long as I can remember and I feel privileged to have a ringside seat at its destruction. Hitler predicted a system that would last 1,000 years and actually it has lasted 12 years, one month, three weeks at this date— and our troops are in complete control of Germany west of the Rhine and east of the Oder.

I mentioned that I visited Aachen. I should like to see someone propose that the destroyed city of Aachen be left just as it is—a great wall should be erected around it, and admission charged so that people for all times could come and see what happens to those who try to enslave the world. It is a sight I will never forget. The admission fee could be used for the education of orphaned Dutch and Belgian children just across the border. It would be an object lesson worth a million words—the memorial to tyranny.

Most of the Germans are very meek now, but I don't believe their innocent smiles and am not sorry for any except the tiny ones.

Germany had no sympathy for little children when she conquered.

This whole experience overseas has its good points. I am sure that I shall never regret having come here. The Army at home and the Army abroad are as different as day and night. You get the feeling that here you are making a more direct contribution to victory, a victory that the enemy cannot long delay. If I seem optimistic, that's the way I feel.

We're winning, and I have never been so impressed with the power of our Army. When I can tell you the details, I'll talk you to death.

Passover is coming soon—have a nice Seder. We hope to have one here if possible.

All my love, sweetheart, and keep smiling—just for me.

Your, Harold

P.S. Am enclosing 1 occupation mark (10¢) and 2 franc note (4¢). Don't spend it all in one place.

⌒⇁

Somewhere in Germany
March 26, 1945

Lo Darling,

I've been giving this post-war future a lot of thought. As I saw France, I was not impressed. The French are thoroughly defeated and depressed. The Republique will never attain her former stature—her great leaders—Daladier, Blum, Heriot, are all dead. I don't trust DeGaulle nor do I like him. As for England, the people are fine—we couldn't want finer friends and better allies. But the thing known as Imperial Policy is bound to make Britain play everybody off against everybody else. So while we shall always be bound to England by mutual interests we shall always have to watch the died in the wool imperialists like your pin-up boy Winny because they are Empire first and the rest of us afterward. That leaves the greatest power to be in Europe—Russia. And I do emphatically trust Russia to do her full share to keep the peace and support the world security organization.

The Soviets are sincerely interested in peace and anxious to do their part. My great hope is that we, as the great power of the West, will work intimately and closely with our Russian allies in the years to come. The security thereby attained will make all our present sacrifices worthwhile. With the British at our side, we shall be invincible and we can enforce peace in our time and our children's time.

I shall be anxiously awaiting letters from you and the folks (damn—the Heinies are jamming our British radio program again).

All my best love to you, adorable—I love you and dream of you, sweet.

Ever,
Your, Harold

⌇

Somewhere in Germany
March 28, 1945

My Darling,

Tonight is the first night of Passover and Sam & I are going to a Seder the Army has arranged. It will be the first free Passover in Germany for 12 long years and I'm thrilled to be able to celebrate it here, especially. I'll write all about it tomorrow.

I'd like to be able to tell you just where and with whom we are in Germany and what we are doing, but our censorship is pretty strict yet. You'll hear it all soon in person I hope.

I started to save parts of Mom's letters and some of yours at one time but it is really impossible. I now burn them.

I got a letter from you, Dad too, of which I'm quite proud since he's about as regular a correspondent as Pop. Tell "Pappie" thanks. I enjoyed hearing from him and appreciate his writing. I guess they all understand that by writing to you, I feel I'm keeping in touch with all the family.

Remember—don't stick around home too much—get out and

enjoy yourself. I am enjoying living in the houses of, and overrunning the country of, the supermen.

Take care of yourself, sweet, and keep dreaming of that not long distant day when we'll be in each others arms again.

With all my love,
Your, Harold

⌒

Somewhere in Germany
March 29, 1945

Lo Dearest,

Sam and I are sitting in our Kraut bedroom burning old letters. I am enclosing a swastika (Hitler Jugend) as a trophy for you.

Almost everything that happens is interesting—the attitude of the ex-supermen who weekly line up in front of American Military Government offices for food and lodgings, the effects of total war on the "sacred" soil of the Third Reich, the perfectly marvelous job the Army is doing. The civilians interest me most. They often seem more puzzled than scared at first. But on the faces of some there is real hatred. It doesn't matter to us how they feel. They are Germans and they will have to live where they are told, keep order, and obey the curfew. All are treated with suspicion and exactly alike. If they have any complaints they can take them to the AMG.

We're all feeling fine and the news every day from all over Germany continues to be excellent. I am no strategist, but I am quite sure the German Army has entered upon the phase of disintegration.

And so, from liberated Germany, a Happy Passover. By the way, I attended a service yesterday in this godawful Germany—a theatre full of Jewish soldiers who celebrated the Passover in a German town that no doubt had not had such a service for at least 12 years. But that happened all over Germany last night—at least liberated Germany—which will soon be all of Germany.

Sam & I have a bottle of Tokay (where from—military secret) so
we shall quaff it. I still don't like the hours in the Army—they should-
n't allow it to get started until 9 A.M. Somebody ought to pass a law!

Terry, Sam, and Joe send their best. And Johnny wanted me to say
hello too. Incidentally, you are now officially with us—one of our
vehicles is named Charlona (Charlotte—Davis' wife), Lo, and Na
(Nadine Philbeck). I'm proud of that name—I thought it up.

With all my love,
Your, Harold

༄

Somewhere in Germany
April 6, 1945

Lo Sweetheart,

The more I see of Germany, the happier I am that Grandma and
Grandpa left for America. There is going to be a terrible fight for sur-
vival after this is over and only the strong will survive. These people
bled all of Europe and have been well fed, well clothed, and well
housed up to now, but the Germans will really be out of luck. No one
in Europe is willing to forgive and forget a single indignity visited on
them during the last few years.

We occupy these countries and step into the homes of these Krauts
and use them as we please, kicking the families out. Lots of homes
have been looted by German soldiers long before we get to them,
which shows a lot of poor morale in the enemy lines.

A very pathetic thing happened a few minutes ago. The Germans
that lived in this house included among them an old man, partly para-
lyzed and not quite right in the head. We were working in the room
assigned to us when suddenly the door opened and the old boy, all
bent over and half blind came in, hung his hat on a nail, and looked
around for a chair. We had rearranged the room, and he couldn't find
it. The interpreter didn't get across what we had to tell him—the family was living in the barn so we had to get another Kraut to take him

away. He's probably living the glories of the Franco-Prussian war in his mind and doesn't know the Fatherland is invaded.

Yes, we have about the same kind of ideas about people and everything. Distance doesn't matter much when you react to everything the same way. That's why I am never very lonesome though I miss you like hell.

April has really been rainy. March was a beautiful month, but now we're getting rain and mud. I'm certainly glad I don't have to live outdoors—at least not yet.

Everything on the fighting fronts is going very well. It's getting to be a race as to whether Patton or Zukhov will make Berlin first.

Regards for everyone—and all my love to you, darling, from your absent but loving,

Harold

Somewhere in Germany
April 8, 1945

Lo Dearest,

I know how much you'd like to know just who we're with, where we are, and what we're doing. I'd love to tell you (we've never had secrets from each other) but the situation is such that I can't. I have been asking when I could, and when they allow it, you'll be among the first to know.

It's a little early yet, but don't forget Mother's Day for both our mothers. I'll send wires in time—at least I hope they'll be in time.

I'm feeling fine—the air is good here even if the natives who breathe it are crumby. I sleep soundly when I can—some days plenty and some not so much. If I were on the other side you wouldn't be hearing from me at all—the Germans have had to suspend their Postal System. There isn't much future in being a German at all, much less a Nazi. As far as we're concerned they're all Nazis.

I suppose you hear all the wild rumors—Goering dead, Hitler

dead—all of which doesn't matter. The German Army is in its death agonies and is now engaged in prolonging them.

The mail is wonderful—I am more interested in your letters than in the news. It really seems like a miracle that our mail has speeded up so much since we've gotten to the continent.

Take good care of yourself, dear, and keep up the letters.

My regards to the gang at the store, and tell the folks in Cleveland I'll write them soon.

All my love,
Ever,
Your, Harold

⌒

Somewhere in Germany
April 8, 1945

Dear Mother and Dad,

Just got two letters—and a package. The package was from you and contained nuts, those little candies, toast, cheese, and sardines. Many thanks. We had a feast last night.

I got a swell letter from Crites yesterday. I always prize his letters very highly as they sound just like "old sourpuss." He's really quite an unusual guy—you don't meet many like him.

I imagine it's more like home with Lo back in Wooster. And I imagine she's glad to be back. I suppose you and she are just having a grand time getting caught up.

You really had quite an ambitious Seder. I'd have loved to taste your matzoth ball soup and gefilte fish. Boy oh boy—I could use a Seder.

John Bruere wrote a nice letter. When Dad has the chance, say hello for me.

Pop, now that you've broken the ice, how about another letter soon. I enjoyed the last one so much.

Everything's fine here—working hard and knocking the hell out of them. If they don't give up pretty soon we shall have the pleasure of turning this whole lousy country into a scrap heap.

I'm going to sign off for now—thanks for the food. We could use more. Please try some chocolate candy this time—how about it?

All my love—ever yours,

Harold

〜

Somewhere in Germany
April 9, 1945

Lo Dearest,

This was one of my big days. We had showers for the first time in ten days. I think it's a rather interesting story how we get them, so here goes.

The Army provides showers at convenient places. They assign you certain days on which your organization goes to this point.

First you go thru a tent in which they have clean olive drabs. Each man gets a new shirt and trousers and a new pair of socks. Then you go to another tent which is heated and has benches, board walks, and footbaths. You undress there and go into the shower room. You are allowed 5 or 6 minutes under the showers, you come out, dress (in your new uniform) and on your way out throw the old one on a pile. It is gone forever. That way the boys stay clean and don't have to worry too much about trying to clean ODs. It works very well, and whoever in quartermaster thought it up is very ingenious.

It's been five months since I've seen you. I know that you're with me every minute, as I am with you.

I meant to tell you to congratulate Donald for me on his great fight. That looked bad, too, but if you never give up you can't be licked.

All my love to you, baby.

Ever,
Your, Harold

〜

Lo Darling,

This is our most beautiful spring day yet.

All this baloney about the special handling of G.I.s makes me pretty disgusted. We will come home with exactly what we went away with—and most of us are dying to tell you swell gals back home the things—good and bad—that we are not allowed to say now. Of course, some fellows won't want to talk about it at all, but then some people are always close-mouthed, as soldiers and civilians. We won't need to be psyched when we get home—we just want to slip into the life we left behind and find our wives and families where we left them.

This year I attended a Seder service in Hitler's one-time Reich. Next year, I think I'll come home for it.

Last night we had quite a bull session on the question of mind reading. Like all such delightful evenings, nothing was accomplished but we enjoyed it.

Radio Berlin seems to be losing its unique sense of humor. I haven't been able to get a single English language broadcast trying to tell the English what jerks the Americans are or vice versa for several days. Maybe they don't think they can come between us. Germany, as you know, is the home of the harmonica, and quite a few seem to have been "liberated" around here from the noise that goes on—or is it music? No—it is noise. What this Army needs is a course in music appreciation.

By the way, my change in the allotment didn't come thru until now and will not be effective until July. I have very little use for money, I haven't had a chance to spend the $50 you sent me, so I'll get by all right.

So far, I still can't tell you which Army we are with, but hope to tell you more soon.

So much for now. All my love to you, sweetheart.

Ever and always,
Your, Harold

⌣

Darling,

How do you like the news today? Pretty wonderful isn't it? Germany will never rise again in our lifetime or that of our children's children. She will be finished as a great power.

Some of the German civilians living near here asked one of our boys who speaks German who would protect them (the Germans) from the Poles and Russians slave laborers after the Army is gone. That's quite a laugh—protect indeed. He told them we are the friends and allies of the Poles and Russians and if there is any help to be given it will be given to them and not to Germans. These Germans have some nerve thinking we are here to protect them. But it's quite an admission from the supermen—to ask the enemy for protection from their ex-slaves. Most of us are all for the slaves—and what they do to the Germans, man, woman, or child, is no concern of ours. They certainly show a lot of fear for "stout-hearted Nazis." Like all bullies, they cry for mercy when they get their just desserts. So gradually that you can hardly tell it, this people is disintegrating and I think the breakdown is going to be a very complete one.

I hope I'm not boring you with these anecdotes about the civilian population but that's about the only kind I can pass on, and besides the actions of these people interests me.

Be good, and—I love you.

Ever,
Your, Harold

Lo Dearest,

I was on duty last night when the awful news came in about the death of the President. I couldn't believe it, and even now, 12 hours later, realization comes hard. We haven't gotten any details yet except that he died at Warm Springs, Georgia, of a cerebral hemorrhage.

This is bad news for us all. The great broad vision of Mr. Roosevelt is needed, or rather was, more at this time than ever before. The war is almost won, but his leadership in our behalf at the peace table would have been invaluable. Our hope is that he has been able to inculcate his ideas into the Administration. Mr. Truman starts with a severe handicap and I wish him well. He will be judged by most incompetent even today, but he must have a fair trial. If he listens to those who surrounded President Roosevelt, especially on foreign affairs, he ought to get along.

I have been thinking all the way back to the time when he was Governor Roosevelt—the 1932 campaign—his inauguration which I heard sitting on my day couch in D-12 Kirkland House, and all he has accomplished since. Remember the innumerable times we sat in our den on Scovel Avenue and listened to his marvelous voice? We were privileged, I think, to have lived during the presidency of such a truly great man. America is not Germany, and we shall be able to carry on what he fought and died for just as smoothly as if he were still alive. But we should not have been so well off if he had never lived—his contribution is tremendous and will appear more so in the light of history.

Not only America, but the whole civilized world, mourns his passing. It is a great pity that he could not have lived just a little longer to see his work brought to fruition and had time to relax a few years.

It's going to seem funny—President Truman—but there's nothing funny about the situation. FDR is dead—may his memory live forever.

I haven't written about anything else today—I can't think about anything else. But we shall go on to win—of that I'm sure. And he has left America a heritage of thought that will make us all better citizens.

With all my love,
Your, Harold

↜

Somewhere in Germany
April 14, 1945

My Sweetheart,

Last night we listened to a rebroadcast of the Memorial Program for the late President. Orson Welles made a beautiful talk. They then read telegrams from King George, Premier Stalin, and a host of lesser lights throughout Europe and America. Bing Crosby sang "Home on the Range." Today is a day of mourning at home, we know, and the armed forces have officially gone into mourning. Probably no other death could have been so tragic at this time—as Welles said, "a giant has fallen." The British House of Commons is in mourning and has adjourned until Tuesday. And now it is up to President Truman to do his best to carry out the wishes of the Chief. I know he'll try.

I am enjoying *Yankee from Olympus*. There is a lot more to it than just the life of Justice Holmes and his family. It is a history of the 19th century and is very well written. I think you'd enjoy it—the book is very satisfying. It is a good thing to draw courage in the present from the wisdom of the past.

The war may be pretty exciting, but in each sector there are long periods of inactivity. This gets me down more than anything else. That is our problem in this kind of work. That's why I am starting to read so much. There's really nothing else to do, except read and think ahead to the day when I can be back home and have my darling with me all the time.

All my love, dearest, Harold

↜

Somewhere in Germany
April 17, 1945

Lo Darling,

At last a break in the censorship—I take great pride in telling you we are with the Ninth Army across the Rhine. That is all I can say, but it's more news than I've been able to send you. So just watch the roaring Ninth.

It's hard to picture there's a war going on. I've been sitting in a big overstuffed leather chair looking on a peaceful village street with people quietly walking. In the distance a guy is plowing a field with two mangy looking horses. Everything is very quiet and peaceful. Today I spent a couple of hours at the piano. When I return I should be able to be your private entertainer. I played all our old favorites and spent a lot of time on a tricky arrangement of "Sweet and Lovely." If I say so myself it's not bad.

It's been almost six months since I've seen you, dear. It hardly seems possible. I miss you terribly, every day. I am not in danger—not nearly as much as I could be bustling across Broadway on a New York trip. Sometimes I wake up in the night and it almost tears me apart to realize that I am so far from you. But I always bring myself to the realization that it isn't forever, and I shall be home again. Everything depends on how long the war lasts and what happens afterwards over here. But whatever it is, don't worry.

I didn't get much sleep last night, so I'll sign off early. Besides Terry wants to discuss our favorite subject: How soon will they let us go home. The theme song is "Show Me the Way to Go Home."

Ever,
Your, Harold

P.S. I love you.

Somewhere in Germany
April 17, 1945

Lo Darling,

I just finished writing to Dean Weimer, expressing my feelings as to the death of the President and urging him, as a leading New Dealer at home, to keep up the fight. I have a very special request. Would you please send $50 from you and me to the Infantile Paralysis Fund at Warm Springs as a token of our personal feelings? I imagine there will be a Roosevelt Memorial Fund.

We heard President Truman this evening and I think he made a very sensible speech. If he keeps his head, I'm sure he'll get along OK.

I see where Hitler's order of the day is rather desperate. There's no future in being a German. Wasn't that odd that Radio Tokyo actually praised FDR? Wonder why. Trying to soften us up for the peace per-haps? I'm really starting to wonder if that one will really last too long.

And the capture of Von Papen is another ironic twist from the enemy point of view, unless he actually wanted to be captured. Who knows? We've got them on the run—there's not doubt about that. It certainly can't be long.

What are you doing now, honey? Every day I try to picture what you're doing at that moment. How thankful I am that we had those two years together in the Army. My only morale builder is the knowl-edge that you are waiting for me.

My love to the folks,

Always, all my love,
Your, Harold

⤳

My Sweetheart,

We've really had April showers today. Just like Ohio—if you don't like the weather, just wait 15 minutes.

I want to describe the place we're living in. We're in an apartment building, a modern, middle class one—five stories high. Each floor has two apartments. We're on the 3rd floor. I have a separate room, Les Myers has one, Terry & Don Lundsgaard have the master bedroom, and we have a common living room, kitchen, and bath. From my window I can look down the gabled street of an old world town (name withheld by order of CO). Our office is next door in an ex-tavern— the bar is still there. Joe and his gang are actually cooking in what was a German restaurant across the street. The battery controls two hotels and this apartment and we're all very comfortable. The people we "displaced" had a pretty nice place. By looking at them you can tell they were the more prosperous class. The policy of the Army is to take the best homes available for the troops. One thing has struck me as rather funny—you have always wanted to live in an apartment, but it was I who finally made it. In fact, it's not all bad, and the way we live reminds me of college days at Kirkland House. We work 12 to 15 hours a day seven days a week, but who cares—no where to go anyhow.

There's only one thing that keeps it from being fun—that's no you. And I've never had a good time anywhere without you.

Until tomorrow, good night, my love.

Ever,

Your, Harold

9th Army, Germany
April 23, 1945

Lo Dearest,

Today, I took a bath! All these German towns have bath houses. Each customer gets a private room with a tub full of hot water. You provide your own soap and towel. The cost is 70 *pfennigs* (7¢). The price is well worth it.

The Russians are making the news now. Their drive thru Berlin is really going to flatten the town. I'm glad they got there first.

In a couple of days the San Francisco Conference will open. The whole world will be watching and practically all will be wishing them well.

How's Mother's wrist? I do hope she's coming along OK.

With all my love—forever dearest.

Your, Harold

〰

9th Army, Germany
April 25, 1945

My Darling,

My piano technique has improved quite a bit since I've had access to one. It is a beautiful piano. "Deep Purple" is one of the boys' favorites, along with "Stardust," "Shanty in Old Shantytown," and lots of songs. The old ones remind us all of home and we don't hear many new ones. Our Armed Forces Network (A.F.N.) Programs feature mostly the old sentimental favorites. Is that true in the States too?

Up until now German civilians did without little. Most of the women wear silk stockings. They've had plenty of food, good clothes, nicely furnished homes. The war left them short of very few civilian goods until they lost it. Naziism and the organized looting of Europe's goods and labor market paid healthy dividends to the German people.

For once I agree with a recent article stating that the German people didn't oppose moral objections to Naziism and materially benefitted from it, hence should be willing to share its fate.

I love you dearest,
Harold

⤶

Somewhere in Germany
9th Army
April 26, 1945

Lo Dearest,

The first newspaper for German civilians (printed in German by our authorities) appeared today. All the Germans were anxious to see it since most of them haven't read a paper or heard the radio (electric power out most places) in weeks. The expressions on their faces was most interesting. The younger ones obviously disbelieved the headlines, "Reds Fighting in Heart of Berlin," and dismissed the whole thing as Amerikanische Propaganda. The older ones were very thoughtful. After a few days of the truth even the most ardent Nazis among these youngsters will realize their New Order has crashed about their ears. At the place where the papers were distributed by G.I.s, they mobbed the boys to get them. It is pathetic to see how insulated they have been from the truth. We will use truth, thru these papers, to start to break into the minds of these people. I can't get used to such a civilized and healthy looking people being so terribly primitive about the real issues. They have no idea how they are hated by us and our allies but they are finding out.

I must tell you the stove story: A German who spoke a little English came to our apartment to get some things. It is OK for them to take food, clothing, and personal things. But anything that we can use, especially heavy stuff like furniture, they can't have. This guy wanted to take out the stove and we told him—*Nein.* But I have a wife and child he said. Well, he was told, the Poles had children too. We aren't living in your house because we want to—we'd rather be home. There's more to it than that, but that illustrates how cocky these Krauts are even in defeat. The lesson they must learn will be hard to teach them.

Hope you like the Basement. Lots of action and it's a friendly department. It's a good set up for you and I know you'll like it. Good luck.

And good night, Snooky.
Harold

∽

9th Army, Germany
April 27, 1945

Lo Darling,

We've had quite a week here. Our first issue of Cokes came in and I had my first Coke since I left the States. Almost like home for a moment. Last night we saw *Laura*, a pretty good mystery picture. We have taken over the State Theatre in this town and we really have a beautiful place for movies.

This is beautiful country. I miss you. There is a lovely old castle surrounded by a moat in the neighborhood, a perfect Gothic. I miss you. The people present a very interesting study as the realization of their defeat dawns slowly. I miss you. The gang is all well and I couldn't bunk up with a better gang than Terry, the Myers boys, Sam, and Lundsgaard—we have swell times together. I miss you. I'm still reading *Yankee from Olympus* and working on accounting. I miss you. In other words, I miss you, darling. In all my life I've never missed anyone so much. Yet I feel I've always been with you this last six months.

I'll write more tomorrow.

Ever,
Harold

∽

Lo Darling,

It is a bright sunshiny day but much colder than we have at home. It surely should warm up soon. We now have electricity in our apartment.

The war goes on. At first I had expected that before we had gotten as far as we have, the Germans would surrender. I think I see why we are being forced to fight into the last battlefield in this war. This cannot be measured by ordinary standards, especially by those of the last war. It is not Germany we are now fighting but National Socialism. The Nazi Party can be historically compared to the Jacobins of the French Revolution. We of the 20th century are confronted not so much by war as by the clash of two revolutionary ideologies—Fascism and Communism. We of America and the British Empire are more allied to the latter, mainly because in the 25 years since the Communists found "their country" in Russia, they have abandoned world-wide revolution as an ideal while the Fascists, who found "their country" in Germany, have not abandoned this ideal. The resistance we shall meet in the so-called "National Redoubt" in southern Germany will not represent Germany nor the German High Command. It will represent the Nazis, just as the revolutionary French armies of 1790-94 did not represent France but the Jacobins. It makes no difference that the Jacobins were successful and the Nazis were not. They are both motivated by a religious fervor in their cause, even though the French revolutionaries were ultimately interested in "liberty" and the German in "order." For Hitler substitute Robespierre, for Goering, Danton, for Goebbels, Marat. Substitute the German efficiency for French energy—and you have the French Revolution grotesquely repeating itself, in another key and with opposite lyrics. This whole thing is inexplicable without realizing that we are confronted with the dying gasp of an unsuccessful revolution. Wars die when the diplomats take over from the generals—and they die all in a moment. Revolutions die when the revolutionaries die, and usually they imbue the next generation with some of their ideas, even in unsuccessful revolutions such as the National Socialist. It had a tremendous hold on the people of Germany, and more on the rest of Europe. It will not completely die in our time. The opposing "religion" of Communism is all there is in Europe to offer these people left in a vacuum by the "death" of Nazism, if it will die. You don't kill ideas with guns. You kill them with other ideas. Can we implant in the people of Europe, our ideal of a free society with new necessary economic controls (the New Deal) as an ideal to replace the one we are putting in the shade? If we can, we can win the peace.

Enough of the "philosophy of the State" as Earnest Hocking at Harvard used to call this kind of stuff. But I was surprised it took me so long to realize the character of struggle we are in. The armed part of it is about over—the real war, the one of ideas, is about to begin. So far we are still on the defensive. Let's hope San Francisco will not present formulae so cold as to leave us without hope.

And please save this letter, honey. Ten years from now I want to see whether I was right or wrong about the fundamental character of World War II.

My love to everyone, snooky, but particularly to my own darling.

Ever, Harold

⤴

9th Army, Germany
April 29, 1945

Lo Darling,

This is a gloomy Sunday afternoon, no place to go, nothing to do.

To continue what I was talking about yesterday, in comparing the Nazi with the Jacobin of the French revolutionary days, I think we in America, and the people of the British Commonwealth, are faced with a peculiar dilemma. The proponents of these two 20th-century faiths—Naziism and Communism—are followers of a new faith, inspiring perhaps as much by its very newness as by anything else. We, of the Western democracies, had our revolutionary period before Napoleon's time—we are the spiritual inheritors of the French Revolution. In its day that Revolution—with its slogan of Liberté, Egalité, Fraternité—was quite as exciting as the slogans today of the newer revolutions. And ours was successful too. But with the passage of decades and centuries, usage wears out words, and the humdrum of everyday practice tarnishes ideals. So we have the advantage of a successful "going concern" without the do-or-die enthusiasm of the others. The big job is to revitalize democracy and make it look not new, but beautiful. We must sell it to Europe and Asia—if we can't, somebody will sell them something else. And that will make this war useless. But if by example and help we can plant the seeds that grew in Western Europe and America 175 years ago, it will have been eminently worthwhile.

Now I shall get busy on my accounting work. Thank God for it—it keeps me from going nuts.

With all my love, darling, ever to you.

Your, Harold

P.S. Radio just reported Mussolini was executed. That's poetic justice, especially since it was done by Italians.

〜

9th Army, Germany
May 1, 1945

Lo Dearest,

It's May Day and the Red Flag of Russia flies over the Reichstag, and Italy surrendered. The old 69th (Bolte's Bivouackin' Bastards) of Camp Shelby has achieved immortality by being the first division to meet the Russians. German resistance is coming only from SS or Gestapo troops—the Army has practically thrown in the sponge.

We are at the very threshold of victory in Europe. Everyone in the ETO is sweating out the who, what, why, and wherefore of what next. China-Burma-India? Occupation? Home? No one knows. We shall just have to wait. We do know they will let us know what our fate is to be as soon as possible after V-E Day.

I'm quite sure that if they use the point system I am still going to be in the Army for some time to come. A great deal will probably depend on the fate of this outfit—where it goes after V-E Day. At the moment we know nothing.

Remember when the police used to chase the communists on May Day? On the front today Russians and Americans of all ranks are celebrating the Communist Day with vodka and whiskey. Three cheers for the Soviet Union!

With all my love, Harold

⌒

9th Army, Germany
May 3, 1945

Lo Darling,

I am sending you a snap taken while en route to this place from "somewhere in England." From left to right—Bernie Snyder, Ray Bowman, and yours fondly. The jeep is the one named partly for you—you can read "*Char Lo Na*" on it. Sorry. I didn't smile for you. Also sorry I still can't tell you where I was stationed since leaving New York. Sounds silly to me, too, but that's how it is.

Isn't the climax in Europe wonderful? Posters are up all over Germany showing the Germans what they have done—graphic pictures of the scenes in concentration camps. These propaganda drugged people look at them but don't believe it. After they have it drilled into them for a few years maybe they'll wake up.

Every few hours something new—Hitler dead, Goebbels a suicide, Berlin fallen, Hamburg won, North Italy surrendered—this is finally the collapse of the great German machine. Thank God.

Almost time for the news—I wonder what cowardly Nazi leader has jumped off the bridge tonight.

With all my love,
To my bestest gal, Harold

〜

9th Army, Germany
May 7, 1945

Lo Darling,

This is a "pins and needles day." We are waiting hourly for the end. Everybody is pretty excited. There will be a hell of a celebration when it happens. Of course it isn't all over—but we'll be on the home stretch.

Well! Thank God! The news just came in—7:30. The war in Europe is over. It was just announced at A.F.N. (Armed Forces Network) that fighting has ceased and by 3 tomorrow afternoon all German armed forces will be formally surrendered to the United Nations. This is Der Tag for us. Two down, one to go. I am wondering how long the Japs will hold out all alone after seeing Germany's fate. They seem very hurt at Germany's surrender.

I feel quite choked up and very thankful tonight. It was a long road—at first it seemed impossible. Once again freedom has won over a tyranny that caught her unprepared. So that is that. Now I am ready to see what happens—and I am ready to come home for good. Of course, there is the little matter of the Army point system and the fact that I have been overseas less than 5 months.

For today the end of the war is enough. Let's hope to God never again.

That's all I can say tonight. I just got a letter from you written when you got to Cleveland. I think it's a swell idea for you to go back and forth. It does you and everybody good.

I love you, Harold

〜

9th Army, Germany
May 8, 1945

Lo Darling,

This is a beautiful day—just as if nature realized the war is over. We just listened to President Truman speaking from Washington, making the official proclamation of peace in Europe. It is a wonderful day, and I can just imagine how everything is at home—I can see Euclid Avenue and Times Square—and hear the radio on North Bever and Cumberland Road. The war in the West is over.

We are having a little party here tonight—nothing elaborate, but just a battery celebration. There will be thousands of them.

In a few days I am sending you some war trophies—a Nazi captain's hat, a Nazi party emblem, and a large swastika.

Well, now that it's official, we are sweating it out. Don't know what to expect, but we hope for the best.

Soon we should be able to tell you gals all the dope—where we are, where we were, what we're doing.

The "lights are on" all over Europe tonight. And I love you very much and am so proud you're mine.

Ever, Harold

9th Army, Germany
May 9, 1945

Lo Darling,

This is another lovely spring day. The kind that made me sit down at the piano and tinkle out Rubenstein's "Melody in F." I did pretty well too, thank you.

We had a beer party last night in honor of V-E Day, and I understand there is to be some champagne and cognac tonight. Even though the war is not over by any means, the end of it in Europe will certainly simplify things.

I just got a letter and package from your mom—some olives, kado-ta figs, soup, and cocoa-malt.

I imagine I'll soon be able to tell you the town we're in. I don't know why they haven't relaxed the censorship. At any rate, it's a beautiful little old world town—I'd just love to take you by the hand and stroll thru the crooked streets, flanked by the ancient and picturesque three and four storied, gabled houses. I get "powerful" lonesome for you, baby.

With all my heart—I adore you,

Harold

9th Army, Germany
May 14, 1945

Lo Darling,

This is an experimental letter—I don't know whether it will be cut—but I'm going to tell you a few things I haven't been able to so far, as censorship is relaxing.

In England we were stationed at Hereford, in the west, not far from the Wales border. We were in lovely country. We were close to the great Cathedral town of Gloucester, a two-hour ride from Cardiff, and very near Worcester, which I was dying to mention to you. I was allowed to tell you about our trips to Birmingham and London.

After we crossed the Channel we were stationed during our very short stay in France. Our camp was located near the city, on a high bluff overlooking the Seine—you could see miles of beautiful French countryside rolling on both sides of the wide river. I sat on the bluff for hours just gazing out at La Belle, France. After leaving Rouen, we followed the historic invasion route to Germany—Charleroi, Liege, Belgium—and though we were months after liberation, people shouted, waved, and cheered. Just before entering Germany we passed thru a corner of Holland. Since being in Germany I have seen the ruins of Aachen, Munchen-Gladbach, Luitfort, and Dortmund. I can't yet tell you where we are now stationed.

Here's the part that you've been wondering about—we came over to Scotland on the Queen Elizabeth six days from New York. A lovely ship—one of the world's largest. We left New York harbor the early morning of December [CENSORED].

I love you.
Your, Harold

⌒

9th Army, Germany
May 14, 1945

My Darling,

I wrote a letter telling about our location in England and France, the first break in the censorship.

There was so much in Hereford you would have enjoyed. The beautiful, neat countryside of Herfordshire—thatched cottages, stone walls dating back to Rouen days, the old cathedral and the crowds in "High Town" (as they call the center of town) on Saturday afternoon. Hereford is a small town (about 35,000). There are a couple of wide streets, but in the center of town the streets are narrow and crooked with picturesque houses and overhanging second floors that remind you of the steel engravings on Christmas cards.

We were located 7 miles from the city for over two months. I liked Hereford. The American Red Cross Club was run very well. The people were grand and hospitable. I shall never forget Hereford (pronounced by the British—*Harry-ford*). It was almost like leaving home when we pulled out March 5th. We drove to Southampton (which really got some bombing earlier in the war). We landed at LeHavre after crossing the channel on a Liberty Ship and drove to Rouen. Rouen was very badly damaged—a shambles, but we did do some sightseeing—including the cathedral courtyard where Joan of Arc was condemned by the English to die at the stake as a witch during the Hundred Years War. But soon we left for the front which was then the

Rhine. We passed rapidly thru northern France, Belgium, and a tiny corner of Holland—then across the border into Germany. One day later we crossed and worked around the Ruhr, mostly in small towns around a place called Recklinghausen, north of Dortmund. I'm not going to be anymore specific just yet. Now you have a good idea of my odyssey so far.

Tomorrow, after a further check with the censor, I'll try to tell you the story of our trip across the bounding main.

Someday, I want to show you some of the things I've seen.

So, until tomorrow, auf wiedersehen, my love.

Ever,
Your, Harold

P.S. Japs or no Japs—every day is one day nearer victory—and you.

∽

Detmold, Germany
May 16, 1945

Lo Darling,

I don't believe I've mentioned much about our "charming" Germans recently. The people are now trying so hard to be friendly. They beam at you, the girls (and they are mostly pretty) smile invitingly, and the children all come up to pat our dog Rusty. They look at Old Glory flying outside our buildings and seem (on the surface) to approve. They are putting on a great act—the same act they put on after the last war and it worked then. They are now trying to convince us, and thru the armies the peoples of the United Nations, that Germans are really a very friendly, cultured, charming people, that this "unpleasant business" was caused by only the Nazis ("of course most of us were not Nazis"), and that the Western world for its own good must realize the extent to which Germany is essential in the post-war world.

But it won't work this time, thank God. We shall not forget Buchenwald and Dachau, the steel whip and the club, the starving of allied PWs and treatment of the conquered nations which we regard as part of the famous German Kultur. That is why we have this much discussed and very difficult policy known as non-fraternization. It is all-inclusive and forbids any contact with any German man, woman, or child except in line of duty. Naturally there are violations, particularly as regards the Frauleins and G.I.s. The punishments are heavy and yet you can't expect some fellows to obey these rules. But for the most part it will have the desired effect—to demonstrate to Germans that all of them are held responsible for the crimes of this country and they must be considered as unfit for normal human beings to associate with for a long time while they prove to the world they can live in peace. And that is the reason for non-fraternization.

I agree with you that Mr. Truman has made a very auspicious start. I do think, however, he is to be criticized for a couple of his appointments—at least one appointment seems to smack a little of the Harding "old crony" kitchen cabinet, but it is too early to be sure. I just hope he is not too prone to allow personal loyalties to interfere with good appointments.

Today's *Stars and Stripes* carried a story about the war with Japan being expected to last 1-1/2 to 2 years. If the Russians come in (and I'm convinced they must in order to protect their Pacific interests) with the British in the South Pacific, I think we shall win much more quickly. Within a very short time the Japs will get blows they can't hope to protect themselves from. I wouldn't like to be a Jap. And watch our Chinese allies get rolling now that we can equip and support them properly.

It is a very heartening thing that we, the most peace-loving and democratic of all nations, have built the world's most powerful war machine and equipped the rest of the free world besides. Our top leadership in all theatres is simply superb. Very few American boys have died needlessly. Our staff offices are the world's best—all from a war-hating democracy. I guess it's not for nothing that the Yankees of

Revolutionary times used a flag with a serpent on it and the motto: "Don't Tread on Me!"

Our enemies are learning the hard way that our "easiness" is deceptive and no one had better fool around with this "decadent democracy."

It's a beautiful spring evening. It stays light until 10 o'clock—Double British Summer Time—seven hours faster than yours. I wish I had you here tonight.

I love you, darling—
Always, Your, Harold

∽

9th Army
Detmold, Lippe
Germany
May 18, 1945

Darling Lo,

This morning I took a ride with Sam thru the countryside. We went thru some of the most beautiful country I have seen—rolling hills and neat little farms, without an inch of wasted space. Of course I haven't been in South Germany, but all I've seen of it between here and Aachen leads me to believe it was a very beautiful country before the war. It's a shame these people can't learn to behave themselves—they have such a beautiful place. Wherever you go you are greeted by smiles and the little children wave gaily from the roadside—how quickly they've changed tactics! It's almost unbelievable and you have to see it to appreciate it.

I'm taking German lessons now. There is a teacher in Detmold who gives lessons to those of us who are interested—one hour a day. You have to get permission to take them. It's very interesting, and I'm enjoying it. The teaching material is not the same as that used in our schools. You learn by phrases—words of greeting, asking directions, ordering food and drink. Gradually, by imitating the teacher, you can approximate the German pronunciation. I am surprised at the number of words I recognize—from way back when Grandpa was alive. And I seem to have trouble only with the most difficult vowels as far as pronunciation is concerned. This course is not designed to teach us to speak the language, but to be able to understand and express ourselves when necessary. You don't talk to Germans except in the line of duty. If Grandpa were alive he'd get a kick out of watching me try to form my mouth (round, *plizz*) for a long ö or ü. Sam is taking it too and we study together.

Still waiting and hoping for the best and keeping my fingers crossed. I'd cross my toes too if it would bring me one minute nearer to you. The more I see of the world, the more I want only you—

Forever Your, Harold

⌐

Detmold, Germany
9th Army
May 19, 1945

Baby Darling,

At last they've stopped unit censorship and I can be free in what I write you. I've been a little reluctant to really let myself go when these officers whom I see every day read my mail.

Now for the details that need to be filled in since I left. On December 6 we left Shelby on a special train and 48 hours later arrived at Camp Shanks, Nyack, New York. That is the Port of Embarkation. While there we were given shots, checked on records and clothing.

On the evening of the 15th we were alerted and loaded on trains, we crossed the Hudson on a ferry, and boarded the HMS Queen Elizabeth at Pier 60 North River. It was the same pier from which we sailed on our honeymoon. A nice piece of irony. The pier had only MPs and Secret Service men on it and a band which played "Over There" about 1,000 times.

Everybody was confined below decks until the middle of the next day.

We actually sailed at 5 A.M., December 16, 1944. When we came out on deck all we could see was a last tip of Long Island in the distance.

The Elizabeth is one of the two or three largest ships in the world. It has eight decks. Naturally we didn't live in luxury. It wasn't too bad, but quite crowded. Strict blackout was enforced.

We didn't have any trouble in crossing. The biggest problem was eating. They had five sittings in the enlisted mess, and the corridors (gangways) were jammed practically all day with troops waiting for the call.

The crossing took 6 days—we anchored in Glasgow harbor at 1 A.M., December 22nd. We were taken to the dock later in the morning and boarded waiting trains just outside. Then we rode all day thru Scotland and western England—passing thru Glasgow, Leeds, Birmingham—and arrived at Hereford at 1 in the morning, December 23rd. This was our house until March 5th. On that day we left for Southhampton, then to France. We crossed into Germany near Aachen March 18th and crossed the Rhine on a pontoon bridge, after which we participated in the battle of the Ruhr.

I have kept and just reread your letter to me on our anniversary. Any man who has a girl like that will never be really discouraged. What I'm coming back to is well worth waiting for. All I can say is—

I love you and I'm yours forever

—Harold

ᔕ

Detmold, Germany
May 21, 1945

Lo Dearest,

After an utterly beautiful Sunday, we have had rain all day.

We are part of the XVI Corps and are working on DPs (Displaced Persons). We and other outfits round up Russian, Polish, French, Dutch, Belgian, and Italian slave laborers, separate them, and screen them to make sure no Nazis have slipped in. Prisoners of War (that is Russian soldiers) are separated from civilians, and we have the job of finding these various groups places to live until they can be sent home. I don't believe I should go into much detail about it at this time—a lot of interesting human stories and sad tales blossom almost every day. There are 5,000,000 DPs in Germany alone!

Your V-E Day reaction was perfect—we both were lifted but when V-J Day comes we can really let loose.

I love you, rosebud, and absence has only meant I can hardly think of anything else. G'nite.

Your, Harold

⌒

Detmold, Germany
May 30, 1945
Memorial Day

Lo Darling,

I got a letter from you yesterday dearest dated May 23rd. You were naturally disappointed in the series of events leading to the general election in England, but remember that this test was forced by a combination of domestic circumstances. The Labor Party feels that now is the time to set the stage for social and economic reform. Churchill to us symbolized Britain's rugged defiance of the German monster, but he is more than that. He is also a Tory, a Conservative, and a big Empire man who is devoted more to the glory of the welfare of Britain.

Did you see the May 28th issue of *Time*? The 37th got a nice write-up. We fought in the Ruhr with one division mentioned there—the 79th (Cross of Lorraine). In fact I attended Passover services with the "Cross" boys, their Jewish chaplain conducted it. He calls himself the only Rabbi who proudly wears a cross. All of these outfits have a lot of pride in their accomplishments and pay for them in blood. As Corps troops we never make the headlines, but Headquarters Battery 219th didn't have a single man or officer killed, wounded, or missing in 50 days straight in the combat zone.

We may be occupation—if so, the Pacific is out, and so is home until V-J Day. But only 400,000 out of 3,500,000 are staying here and lots of them will be outfits with too much combat service.

I do expect a period of two or three more months special policing, then redeployment orders for eventual Pacific duty via U.S. and 30-day furlough, then a training period in the States (of 3 or 4 months duration), and then—it will be almost a year from now—either shipment to the Pacific or strategic reserve. The only situation that would be hard to handle would be the slim outside chance of direct shipment to China-Burma-India and that too would take at least six months.

It's getting late, so I'll kiss you goodnight and dream of holding you tight at the earliest opportunity.

Your, Harold

Detmold, Germany
June 1, 1945

Hello Sweetheart,

Tonight the Royal Air Force brought the Royal Squadronaires to the Theatre. They are, in peace time, one of London's top dance bands, and they gave us two solid hours of music—the latest American music, and lots of jive.

Well, we're in our last two days in Detmold—and then we move south to Fulda. It's all Germany to us.

Today we took a Hitler Jugand leader to the War Criminal Camp at Sennelager. Snyder and Babbit and I—three Jews taking a Nazi to his death. I'll sleep well tonight—I did a pleasant duty. I must tell you all about Sennelager—when I see you. Briefly it's a concentration camp for war criminals only and it's run by the Dutch. All who enter there are doomed to the same treatment they meted out. We took a long walk around and took some pictures of the place. The guards all carry tommy guns and aren't afraid to use them. The prisoners work about 8 hours a day and stand motionless at attention. They are not tortured, but they have only this rigid grind to face until they die—and if they get out of line they die more quickly—nobody cares. There are hundreds of such camps in Germany and they have quite a few permanent (and I mean permanent) guests and it's only the beginning. The rules of the Geneva Convention do not protect war criminals. I enjoyed my visit and the hospitality of our Dutch allies—our Jugand man will soon find out how much crime pays—the guards will see to that. They were all prisoners themselves 2 months ago. There are 300 Gestapo women prisoners in a separate compound and they get the same rough treatment from husky women guards the men get from the Dutch. They who lived by terror shall die by terror is the motto.

All my love, baby, and a long kiss.

I love you, Harold

⤺

Detmold, Germany
June 2, 1945

Lo Darling,

We packed up today to move to Fulda. Seems like old times in combat—trucks loaded, duffel bags on them, everything ready to take off in the morning. It's much more leisurely now than then—in those days we often moved on an hour's notice.

We've been in Detmold since April 20th and this is the first town since Hereford where the streets are familiar. Leaving Europe (if headed in the right direction) is all I'm really looking forward to now.

Sam and Terry thought that being over 35, they might soon get out but I see the War Department has put a damper on that. Oh well, for most of us that is too good to be true.

The Ninth is all over northern Europe now, Belgium as well as Germany.

By the way, the "old man" looks just the same in his pictures.

The more I get around, the broader his philosophy is by comparison with a lot of so-called big shots who won't be able to earn a living if they give up their commissions. I'm not speaking of my immediate officers, but there are some who could stand plenty of inspection and a lot of them are overrated with leaves and bars. There are good ones too, but too many take advantage of their rank.

Terry wants me to join him for a beer, so I'll quit for tonight. I'm feeling fine and dandy. Your pictures show me you're in good health.

All my love, sweetheart,

Your Lonely, Harold

⌒

Fulda, Germany
June 4, 1945

Hello Snooky,

Well, here we are in Fulda. We made the trip yesterday but I was so dog tired last night that I had one of my rare misses and didn't write you. It was a gorgeous Sunday, and we put the top of the truck down and really saw the country all the way from Detmold. Two big cities were in our route—Paderborn, which is a perfect German city—hardly a house left standing—and Kassel which isn't much better. The approaches to Kassel are really gorgeous. You come down a long hill, and there in the valley below is the city, spread out for several miles at the foot of a long, low mountain that stands up behind the city like an unraised loaf of bread. In the center there is a slight depression, and in it sits the white castle that gives the city its name. It's positively beautiful and it takes your breath away. I don't like Germans or want to have anything to do with them, but they have an absolutely gorgeous country. I've been impressed since I certainly didn't come here to enjoy myself. I admired the scenery 15 years ago and I am just as impressed now.

We have pretty nice quarters in Fulda, a much larger town than Detmold. Sam, Terry, and I are bunking together. We have to heat water to shave but on the whole it is quite comfortable. We are living in three-story duplex apartments on the edge of town. Fulda boasts a G.I. "Donut Dugout," a swimming pool, laundry, soda fountain, and a shower unit. So we should be clean, well-fed, and comfortable. I have no complaints so far as our location is concerned except I don't think the move is geographically one mile nearer Ohio.

Tell Pop that I know he's looking forward to my return but he couldn't any more than I, and that I shall have patience as I realize that war is one of the few things in this world where there are really no refunds, exchanges, or rebates. The sooner you resign yourself to taking it all as it comes, the better you feel and the quicker it will be all over.

The food has been arriving. Another box of your food would be very much appreciated.

I think we should realize that total victory is not going to bring Utopia, but rather we should only expect improvement in line with the failings of human beings. The situation in Lebanon and Syria is strictly the clash between imperialism and can be resolved only by power politics. What we as Americans were interested in doing in this war was to make sure that no system of power arose that would threaten us in the conceivable future. The clashes between our allies, and between us and some of them is inevitable, but so long as all parties concerned are willing to compromise it will work out. France is acutely sensitive after 5 years of unbelievable humiliation and she naturally has a chip on her shoulder, but her heart is all right. De Gaulle is piqued but that does not make him a Hitler.

Glad you liked my account of travels to date. Let me know if the base censor ever cuts anything out.

Shall try to send you another news letter soon. For now, that's all, gorgeous—all my love to the best and most fascinating girl in the world.

Ever,
Your, Harold

Fulda, Germany
June 5, 1945

Lo Darling,

Here is another beautiful June day going to waste because we aren't together. The weather has finally warmed up.

Lundsgaard is on pass to Paris and I'm doing the battery clerk work again for a few days. It is kind of fun to get back to it—it's been six months since I had any connection with it at all.

The situation in Syria is quite serious. I rather think both Britain and France are fishing in troubled waters because of the Mosul pipe line which goes thru the area. The French fleet needs the outlet at Beirut for her oiling base, and the British seem unwilling to give up the complete control they have exercised over the Levant for the past five years. Perhaps England is a little worried that France is becoming a Soviet stooge and thus does not want to see that valuable spot indirectly controlled by Russia. Make no mistake about it, there is rivalry in Europe between the huge eastern bloc controlled by Russia and the smaller but more industrially developed Western bloc of powers over which Britain would like control. With Germany non-existent, this is the first time since the days of Ghengis Khan, almost a thousand years ago, that there has been no German buffer between the Slav states in the east of Europe and the Anglo-Latins on the Atlantic coast. For the first time in modern history, Englishmen and Frenchmen are looking the Russian bear squarely in the face without Germany in between. It will be an interesting decade in Europe. I believe the new U.N. security organization will have its first big test over here—and if it fails here in ten or twenty years it will never get a second one. Meanwhile, everybody is acting with remarkable forbearance. It remains to see how they will act when the heat is on in a few years.

I am always thinking of you dearest.

With all my love, Harold

Fulda, Germany
June 6, 1945

Hello Darling,

I'm really glad I haven't gotten a pass to Paris because now I shall get to revisit the "City of Light" in one of her loveliest months. I fell in love with Paris when I first saw her (you can't speak of Paris as an "it"—nothing impersonal about the Montparnasse, Tuilleries, or Champs Elysees), and I'm anxious to revisit the city. Paris is the only city in Europe that was not defiled by the Huns. Not a street name was changed, not a street broadened. Even the Nazi beasts knew that Paris was sacred and didn't touch her. The only fly in the ointment will be going there without you. I enjoyed my memories of the city and have often thought I would like to go there again with you. Perhaps I shall be lucky enough to be in Paris on Bastille Day—June 14th. It will be the first free Bastille Day since 1939 and I imagine it would be an unforgettable sight.

I haven't as yet had a chance to get around Fulda and the surrounding country.

I hope everything is OK at home, and keep your fingers and all ten tiny toes crossed for an early reunion.

I love you always—Harold

June 9, 1945
Fulda, Germany

My Sweetheart,

Today Sam and I were out in the country and got to see a good deal of it. It isn't quite as scenic as it was around Detmold, but it's very pretty. The day was beautiful and we rode in a jeep for mile after mile thru rolling hills and green valleys. Fulda was not a beautiful town before the war. (Detmold was a resort town and this was a textile manufacturing place.) It was heavily bombed and shelled, and chewed-up houses and craters in the street still bear mute testimony to the 8th Air Force and the RAF. They say 40% of this town is destroyed, but people still live in lots of the partially destroyed homes and tenement apartments. The surrounding country looks like Holmes county—farm lands and little picturesque old world villages nestled in valleys. All the houses have red tile roofs and it's quite a nice effect. Today they were haying in the fields. There are almost no men between 16 and 50 left, so women, girls, little boys, and grandfathers do all the work—and believe me they all work. Their men are mostly dead, in PW enclosures somewhere, or have been sent to France, Belgium, Holland, Czechoslovakia, Poland, or Russia to work. Most of the latter will never return. Such is the price Germans will pay for the worship of the swastika. Some will be lucky and will be allowed to come home if they were not ardent Nazis. Germans must be allowed to raise enough food to eat and keep central Europe from becoming a pest hole of disease and starvation. But beyond the bare minimum they shall not get much for decades to come.

To get back to our little jaunt—the country is a little hillier and more scenic than Ohio. Blue mountains fringe the distance and you can see for 10 or 12 miles, with little red-roofed villages dotting the country. It's hard to believe that the people who inherited such a peaceful and beautiful country should be the world's most warlike nation. Well, they won't be in our time again, thank God. Most of the people have seemingly forgotten their sullen resentment of us and are anxious to curry favor—blond frauleins. Grey-haired old folks wave to us and smile as we pass and the little tots (God, German children are beautiful) wave their chubby hands frantically and just can't understand why we usually don't wave back. Sometimes I do—just can't help it. These kids will have a hard enough life to live without making it tough for them now. We are not starving German children. They all get milk and as much nourishing food as is available. The American Military Government takes the stand that the future of this misguided country depends on these blond tots and are determined as soon as possible to start educating them for leadership. The tiny children of Germany are the only Germans that will get a break. So while we, as soldiers, do not fraternize with them (although as average Americans we'd all love to), we at least have the satisfaction of knowing they shall be given their chance to make right what their elders have muffed.

Everybody in this country looks healthy enough, except the DPs we're working with. All Germans have red cheeks, and for the most part they are a very good looking people. The blockade may have affected their diet but they don't look it. I would estimate that it would have taken 20 years to starve them out—Germans ate well down to the end—they were beaten by fire-power, not food.

Still no news as to where we go from here, or in what category we shall be.

You're a tonic to me as nothing else could be—as long as your chin is in the air I'll face the world unafraid.

My love to everybody in Wooster and Cleveland. I can't think of any other way to end this except to say I adore you darling, every moment of my life.

Ever,
Your, Harold

⌣

Fulda, Germany
June 12, 1945

Hello Sweetheart,

I have a terrible time throwing away your letters, so here is what I do once a month. I read them all over again and then burn them ceremoniously. I always save the last one since I would be lost without at least one letter to reread. You've been marvelous about writing, and a month's letters from you alone, let alone from Mother too, make the back section of my musette bag bulge plenty. The mail orderly is as good a friend of mine as the mailman is of yours. Sometimes letters alone are awfully inadequate, but without them I guess we'd go crazy, wouldn't we?

You made a statement in a recent letter that you were interpreting current history as a series of important men dominating the policy and thought of the era in general and of their respective countries in particular. That theory, in history, is known as the individualist theory of history (I'm not so smart—I just read it in Beard's book at 1 A.M. this morning) and a lot of good historians still hold to it. The very opposite of that theory is the so-called Economic Interpretation of History, on which Communist ideology is based, which holds that there is a flow of events carrying men with it and what appear to be the leaders are just the most effective interpreters of what is going on. To these people, Franklin Roosevelt was a great man in the early 20th century but would have gotten no response 50 years earlier. Only those men rise to greatness who can understand and cash in on the trend of the times. The whole argument is something like who came first—the chicken or the egg—I personally don't think either view is entirely correct. True, the man must be in accord with the times, but the leaders of the times help shape its trends. This will make it easier to understand such a man as Marshal Tito, certainly in accord with the times, but pushed by his powerful Soviet friends to get as good a bargain in Adriatic real estate as he can from Western powers (principally Great Britain). Whenever you see Tito, read it as Comrade Tito—that will make it easier.

Don't gather from this that I'm indulging in Red baiting. Nothing could be farther from my point of view. I don't blame Russia for attempting to secure herself as far as possible. She was outlawed by the capitalistic world for 25 years and it is surely naive to expect her to forget all this just because we helped her beat an enemy. Russia is going to be insistent on a pro-Russian Poland, Rumania, Bulgaria, Yugoslavia, Czechoslovakia, Austria, Germany, and Finland. These are her minimal demands. Considering what we are attempting to do in South America to assure our own interests, they are not unreasonable.

The second sphere of influence in Europe will be the bloc of Western democracies. The United Kingdom, France, Belgium, the Netherlands, Denmark, Norway, and such Rhineland areas of Germany as remain in the hands of Britain and the United States will be part of this bloc. Backing it up will be none other than the United States of America. The third bloc will be the American bloc, consisting of ourselves, all the central American states and all but Argentina in South America.

That leaves Asia and the British dominions. By far and away the logical leader of East Asia is China. China's natural position as chief state of Asia is threatened by two things after Japan's fall; first, by the interest of Russia in Manchuria and North China. If Russia comes in with us in the Japanese war in its closing phases, we may expect to see the same type of minimal demands for friendly buffer states made by the Soviet Union in Asia as she is making rightfully in Europe—but I think not so rightfully in Asia. On the other hand, China's hegemony not to say her future also depends on the position the victorious imperialist powers of the West take after Japan's total defeat. These powers, with huge financial interest and colonies and allied satellites in Asia, are Great Britain, the United States, France, and the Netherlands. Between them, they controlled all of east Asia except Siberia, Japan, and China proper before the war. I am sure they will find China will not give them the special right they imposed on her one hundred years ago exactly (Treaty of Tientsin 1845). In this, China will be backed by the U.S.

To peacefully settle all these pressure groups is the job of the new UNCIO. All these conflicting powers have shown that they are anxious—to reconcile them like bargainers in a store—peacefully and over the counter. Don't let anyone tell you that because these conflicts exist that the UNCIO is a failure. If no conflicts existed, we wouldn't need it. So long as all of us are willing to thrash these real problems of sovereignty, imperialism, and economic differences out and will give and take as all the principals did at San Francisco, there is hope for the world. That is what we fought for—not to emerge as a bunch of

Pollyannas all dancing in a circle like a Vassar daisy chain, but to bring about a world where these things can be settled peacefully.

The only thing I can't settle peacefully is the thought that I'm not with you—I'm lonely, and only you can remedy that which you will as soon as I set eyes on you, lovely.

I love you—always and ever.

Your, Harold

↜

Fulda, Germany
June 13, 1945

Hello Darling,

The *Stars and Stripes* is playing up the American reaction to the highly controversial non-fraternization policy. Apparently all the fuss about boy meets girl is shaking the confidence of a lot of the girls back home in their boyfriends and husbands. To me, it is very amusing because the gals who had something to worry about should have realized it before their soldiers ever left the States. The guys who are fraternizing against the regulations in Germany are the same ones who played around in England and France. The crux of the whole non-fraternization issue is that it's simply unenforceable. The fidelity issue is really not the point—the point is they are trying to stop something that those who indulge will never stop doing—any more than prohibition could stop people from drinking. Those of us who don't actually fraternize with the frauleins sneak chewing gum and candy to the kiddies when possible—they're so darned cute and the penalty for that if they want to get rough is just as bad as for drinking, dancing, or sleeping with Germans. They're not trying too hard to enforce any of it. They say they are going to allow fraternization with youngsters. I hope so—I feel very unnatural having to look and see if certain officers are around before smiling at a kid or patting a cute little baby on the head—and Lois, these German children (I have to say it) are darling. And another thing—none of us, even if the more reprehensible forms of fraternization don't appeal to us, would dream of turning anyone in for indulging. I see lots of it but as a non-com I'm blind as a bat and will continue to be so. Far be it from me to attempt to police a fundamental urge—you can't turn back the sea with a pitchfork.

I got a box today with marmalade, olives, and crackers.

Still no news on our category. So far as I know our mail will not be censored unless we're immediately alerted for the Pacific. I don't believe mail from units going thru the States is censored at all until after they are reassembled after furlough. If mail starts to come thru that is censored and I stop talking about coming home, you can guess where we're going. This is just another of my long shot precautions because I feel more and more every day that we are not going to China-Burma-India direct and maybe not at all. I'm very confident that I'll see you before too long.

I miss you and love you beaucoup.

Ever,
Your, Harold

↜

Fulda, Germany
June 14, 1945

Lo Darling,

This is another cold day—I don't think it will ever warm up.

Johnny Philbeck is B.C. again as of yesterday. Captain Grant moved to the staff and we were glad to get Johnny back. He's still a swell officer in my opinion, now tempered by actual combat.

These German people are hard to figure out. We were told they were all so fanatical and such loyal Nazis, but in the 12 years the Nazis were in power, they did such a good job of breaking the spirit of the Germans that they can't even defend their own government. I am getting sick of this "I'm no Nazi" business. To listen to them you'd never guess anybody in Germany ever heard of anti-Semitism and death camps and all the rest of the kultur of this barbaric land.

Oh no, they were all innocent victims of the Nazis—and the Nazis are Hitler, Goering, Goebbels, and Himmler—no others of course. Some admit 10% or 20% were Nazi but no more. These are the people who danced in the streets when Warsaw burned and Rotterdam died and Paris fell. But they're not Nazis. Oh no. The other guy did it all—why blame us—we're innocent.

They employed slave labor—inferiors like Poles, Russians, French, Jews—they beat them and starved them, raped their women and killed their children—but they did it all under orders and they were afraid to disobey. But they're not Nazis. Oh no. I'll never be for a soft peace or for giving the German people a break until the generation now 8 years or older is dead. They are rotten thru and thru. Not only are they brutal, sadistic, murderers—they haven't even got a shadow of the courage of their convictions. They are the sorriest excuse for human beings I've ever seen.

Sure this country will go Communist to a degree. They don't have the political acumen to become a democracy. Maybe in 50 or 75 years it may be—but it isn't now. The Ernst Torglers and Karl Renners will have to take the lead—and Western Europe will be better off than if a weak artificial democracy arises which the Krupps and Thyssens and Junker barons can overthrow for another Hitler whenever the time is ripe. The Junkers and remnants of the Nazis are preparing the third war right now—and they'll get it if we don't see that the social structure on which Germany has been based is destroyed. The people of Germany are hypnotized, so the rest of the world must cut out the cancer which has poisoned Europe for 75 years. The leading business men and landowners (Junkers) of Germany are all war criminals— every single one of them—and should be shot to the last man. If they are not, there will be a bigger blood—letting for our children to face. And the resourceful, mechanically minded German people will follow these bloody leaders this time as blindly as the last—they still don't see what went wrong except that they lost. Sometimes the law of averages will be against us and we'll lose one—and if we ever do, we're thru. I guess that's enough politics for tonight.

There is now talk that we may be in the Army of Occupation. Completely unofficial, but the latest rumor hot off the press. You've been in the Army long enough to know how much or how little it may mean—but it seems to be gaining in strength. I don't know whether I'll be glad or sorry. If it happens, I'll be out of the fighting war definitely but I won't be home for another year. Unless the food situation improves over here, I understand we can't have our wives over. Anyway, the whole thing is indefinite.

Meanwhile, I see you the last thing at night and first thing in the morning. And I always will, darling.

All my love, always and always and always.

Ever,

Your, Harold

~

June 15, 1945

Fulda, Germany

Lo Darling,

Tonight, 6 months almost to the hour since we set foot on the gangplank of the Queen Elizabeth at pier 60 North River, I can tell you what I think is coming for us. Let me warn you that this is not confirmed by anything official, but I personally am quite sure of it.

First, set your fears at rest about the Pacific. We most definitely are not going direct, and if we ever go it will have to be a long, long war. Here's the story. Our assignment has been until now with the Ninth Army. Effective tonight or tomorrow, we, along with the Third, have been redesignated Army of Occupation. The Ninth Army is heading for the States for furloughs, some retraining, and then redeployment to China-Burma-India. The 219th and many like us are now part of the strategic reserve and will be among the last to be redeployed to the States since we are not critically needed in the war against Japan now or in the foreseeable future. Shipping space to the States is for two categories of troops only: first and foremost those who will get furloughs and ship out for CBI and secondly for those being discharged under the point system. In our outfit only four men are being discharged and they will soon be separated from us and sent home. But since we are not scheduled for quick (or probably even likely) shipment to the war theatre we shall have to wait until those in these two priority categories leave until space for shipping can be found for us. That probably will take several months—maybe six. When that time is up, we too will be redeployed to the States as part of what will be by that time the strategic reserve, unless needed and to be shipped into combat. The best estimate I can figure out is that if everything should go wrong in the Pacific we would not arrive there in less than a year's time from now. Frankly I never expect to go there.

Last item for tonight: I went to Jewish services and guess who the Rabbi is—name is Brodie and he's the Rabbi in Hattiesburg, Mississippi. Don't tell me it isn't a small world.

My regards to everyone and my dearest and fondest love to you sweetheart. Good night Snooky dear … sleep tight ….

Ever,
Your, Harold

⌒

Fulda, Germany
June 17, 1945

My Darling,

Today is Father's Day, isn't it? I had not known it until the *Stars and Stripes* mentioned it.

On July 5th the future of Britain will be decided. I am betting on Churchill to win. He will win largely on his war record. If the elections could have been staved off until autumn, I think the Labor Party would bring home the bacon because already Winnie is showing certain weaknesses. For one thing, with the benevolent peacemaker gone with the death of the President, he is having trouble getting along with

Premier Stalin. (Time out—Kelly just brought in the cutest little blond curly-headed baby girl [8 months old] for me to admire. She stretched out her plump little arms and I took her for a moment. Mama waited apprehensively outside the window for us to return her kleine fraulein which we just did. She is such a good little baby, but she wet me a little. If that's fraternization I'm now guilty—and unashamed).

Well, to get back to unimportant matters—Churchill is going to have plenty of trouble with the colonies and dominions too. Australia and New Zealand are not going to snuggle up very closely to the mother country if the Tories are still in control there. Canada is restive too, and South Africa will stick with him only so long as Smuts is alive. I don't mean to intimate the Empire is breaking up, but if England hopes to hold onto it she will have to change with the times, and I'm not so sure she is going to. She will eventually. Having over 3,000,000 Yanks pass thru in the past three years has made a lot of the British think. They'll never get over our "invasion" and Old England will never be the same again. In the post-war years I expect three of the Dominions to become closer orientated with us—Canada, Australia, and New Zealand. All have their own form of New Deal, all are economically swinging into trade with us rather than the mother country, and all basically have more political sympathy for us. A Liberal or Labor government in England will give the UK a chance to hold them more closely but even so "Time Marches On."

There seems to be a lot of talk about our relations with Russia. I don't know who the irresponsible people back home are who talk lightly about our "basic conflict" with the Soviet Union. No G.I. and I'm sure no Ivan wants to fight. We're getting our fill against the Axis. I'm sure the disagreement isn't over here—it must be in some Red-baiting warped mentalities back home. We know well that Russian prowess saved us from many times the casualties here that we might have had and if they want to help us in the Pacific we are more than anxious to fight with them again. While the Russians are undoubtedly building up a set of buffer states for later use, I am quite confident that the fundamental interests of the United States and Russia are not in conflict and will not be unless disturbed by warmongers fishing in troubled waters.

To get back to Britain for a moment, I am very much afraid the British expect our backing in maintaining an equal balance of power on the continent with Russia. I'm quite sure that Congress and the people of the U.S. will not sanction any alliance, either military or political with the British Empire or any other foreign power. I believe we will participate in the UNCIO fully and honestly and that we will maintain our sphere of special influence in Central and South America and our military control in the Central Pacific. Our interest in Europe will be "disinterested good-will," not isolation, but no desire to form part of a European power bloc. Because Britain forced France into an embarrassing situation in Syria and Lebanon (and De Gaulle won't forget it), the time will come when Britain will need allies in the delicate game known as "Who sits on the powder keg." The hope for peace will come not out of secret alliances or military commitments made in advance and secretly, but out of a genuine desire for peace backed up by willingness to sacrifice something for it. If near Eastern oil is more important to Britain and France than peace, then there will be no peace twenty years from now. And if we are not willing to give and take with Russia and China, the peace will again be destroyed when you and I are in our fifties. So it's up to the world now—war is a hell of a mess and in this world you don't give without getting, nor do you get without giving. All the major powers have to be prepared to do a little of both, and maybe a lot, or somebody is going to sponsor another Nazi party under another name somewhere. It won't use the swastika, it may not be anti-Semitic, but it will be a war party and given a chance it will promote another war. No one ever wants war but war will always happen unless nations wake up and realize that so far, in every peace treaty, there is a clause written in invisible ink—the date of the next war. We might lose the next one, so let's hope they leave that clause out this time.

The bombing attacks on Japanese cities certainly are giving the enemy something to think about, and he's only started to experience them. Wait until we send over 2,000 a day. You know the leading German generals and strategists agree that it was bombing that made it impossible for the Wehrmacht to stop us. Japan has more conquered territory but she's spread thinner, and her vulnerable targets are more accessible once we get our bases built up. Her withdrawal from South China means she has given up the New Order in Southeast Asia and the Co-Prosperity Sphere. She will concentrate in North China, Manchuria, Korea, and the homeland. They will all fall, and I'm afraid they will all fight back. But the result is foregone—complete defeat. If Russia comes in and attacks in the north, the most formidable area, Manchuria, may go early. It's too early since V-E Day to speculate on V-J Day, but it isn't too early to say that in another three or four months, when deployment is partially completed, and bases are built, that the Japs will start to get a full taste of what they so foolishly started at Pearl Harbor. And if it goes mile by mile, when it's over, Japan will be ten times as wrecked as Germany is now, and that's bad.

How's the garden coming along? Gee, it was cold late, wasn't it? Even with a late start you should be able to get a good crop. Wish I could help you eat the results. I think of you all the time, darling, and my only thoughts are to get back to you as soon as I can. Be patient, honey, and keep wishing too.

Another box of food came thru yesterday. We really do appreciate them so much. Thanks a million. May we have another? Olives, toast, or crackers and cheese please? Thank you, baby.

I guess that's about all for tonight. With all my devotion, and love, and a million hugs and kisses,

Ever,
Yours, Harold

⌒

Hello Sweetheart,

Well, I finally made it! I am going to Paris on a 3-day pass. The transportation is so slow that I'll be away from duty about a week, since they assure you of 72 hours in Paris. Since it is likely the organization will move in the next week, I may be away considerably longer, wandering up and down Germany in search of the 219th. Terry is going with me and we are really looking forward to doing the town. After tonight I won't be receiving any mail as long as I'm away.

It will be so good to get out of Germany and back on friendly soil. I'm getting so sick of being suspicious of everyone I see and it will just be a warm feeling to be where you feel there is good-will.

As the days go by, I am more than ever convinced that we shall be embarking for home at some not too distant date. After this pass, when I rejoin the outfit, I should be able to tell you more. Anyway, we're all happier about our prospects than at any time since we landed in Scotland. Gee, it seems like a long time since that afternoon back in November when we said goodbye. I'm convinced the worst is over. Once I get back to the States, I'll try to stay. I doubt if we'll be scheduled to leave.

Well, darling, they lifted the ban on non-fraternizing so I'll go outside and talk to your rival Liesl (6 years old). She's teaching me German. Oh yes, the ban was lifted only for children under 8, but that's OK. Liesl is blonde and cute. She must have something important to say because she babbles her curly head off but I don't understand much. She lisps a little. Maybe I'm getting soft—I guess I'd better get out of Germany and let rougher people administer a harsh peace. I'm not really very tough.

With all my love to you—the softest spot in my heart is still yours.

Forever, Harold

Bad Wildungen, Germany
June 19, 1945

Hello Sweetheart,

If the name of the town surprises you, let me explain. Terry and I left the battery on pass for Paris. Our first stop was at this rich little resort town, now a U.S. Army rest center and headquarters of the 78th Infantry Division. We got here at 11 A.M. and have the rest of today to loaf, see movies, lounge at the Red Cross, and drink beer. Tomorrow at 8 o'clock we leave for Verviers, Belgium, by truck. Then tomorrow night we take a train which gets us into Paris. At 7 P.M. that day our pass begins.

We're both already feeling relaxed. We've had a nice lunch (plates too—not mess kits) and a stroll thru town and now we're sitting on a little sun porch. This is my first little holiday since my trip to London. To get away from the Army for a few days is a privilege.

This town has three or four very nice hotels. In a park, there is a nice bandstand with rows of trees extending like the spokes of a wheel in all directions. It is so peaceful and lovely—hard to believe that a war was fought around here—this town is untouched. It makes you realize when you see beauty that something good is in this people, just as you realize when you see homeless children and young girls and old men and women—frightened, without the bare essentials—that it is the weak and poor and helpless who pay for wars in their own ruined lives—the rich and shrewd never do, win or lose.

With all my love, darling,

Ever,
Your, Harold

⤻

My Dearest,

There's so much to say that I really don't know where to begin. Wednesday A.M. we left by truck and arrived at Viviers, Belgium. The trip was hard without incident except for one amusing thing. A quarter of a mile across the border in Belgium, we saw two girls standing by the road and did they get a cheer—the first people to whom non-fraternization didn't apply.

At Viviers we caught the Paris train travelling all night. By the time we got our rooms, it was 5 o'clock. We are in the Hotel De Guiche which is run by the Red Cross. We each have separate rooms—very nice indeed. We eat at a neighboring hotel for 10 fr. (20 cents) a meal. The rooms cost 20 fr. (40 cents) a night. All this is arranged by the Army. The black market here is so awful that a good meal outside would cost 1 to 2 thousand francs ($10-$20). Remind me to tell you about the Paris black market—it's unbelievable: a dress, just a cotton one, costs $75; a pair of shoes, $40; a man's suit, $200; a handbag, $50.

Thursday evening we sat in a café in the Montmarte and watched the Parisiennes strut by. They are easily the most style conscious women in the world and it's a treat to sit at a sidewalk café sipping cognac.

Yesterday we visited a few places such as Place de la Concorde and the Madeleine and late in the afternoon went to the famous Café de la Paix. Then we walked home stopping to enjoy a street carnival. Paree is still the same—they've got nothing to eat, but their hearts are young and gay.

Oh yes, I met a Woosterite. We were walking down the Boulevard de la Madelaine this noon and someone called my name. It was Rex McSweeny, in from Austria on a 3-day pass. He has to leave tonight. He expects to be home in July and says he'll call. Isn't it a small world?

Tomorrow is our last day starting with a tour doing the Eiffel Tower and Luxemborg Gardens. Tomorrow evening we start back to Verviers. I wonder where we'll find the outfit—I'm sure they've left Fulda.

It's hard to put on paper the things you see here or the feeling you have in a city as unique as Paris. It has an atmosphere all its own. The dollar sign is in every eye but you like 'em anyway. Yes, "Paris is a woman's town with flowers in her hair." After the war, someday we'll see this together.

I hope you're well and everything's OK. I miss you more here than ordinarily, sweet, because it would be so much fun for us both to be doing Paris. For me, it's just a welcome change of scenery.

All my love, darling, and here's to being with you soon.

> Ever,
> Always, Harold

P.S. You'd die at the hats here. They are big, high, and mostly out-landish.

∽

> Viviers, Belgium
> June 23, 1945

Hello Sweetheart,

This is the darndest situation. No one seems to know where the 219th is, so we'll stay here at this rest camp until they provide transportation.

This is really a nice spot. The town is lovely—just a small, clean, Belgian city of about 20,000 people. There is a G.I. nightclub, a G.I. theatre, a donut dugout, three G.I. bars, swimming pool, golf course, tennis courts, and a PX. Instead of a three-day pass to Paris, we're going to have at least an extra 3 days at this rest center. The stores downtown seem well stocked with everything from electric irons to cigarette lighters.

It's quite a contrast to Paris. The people are not nearly so well dressed. They have sidewalk cafes here too. And it is something to be out of Germany where people don't look at you as though you personally had killed their whole family. This part of Belgium was very near the Ardennes bulge, but the German drive petered out about 15 miles from here.

Well, Paris is behind me now, and even if it weren't, the only thing I long for is that boat trip home. The hard part about having so much time on your hands here is that you do think of home too much. I love you.

Always, Harold

⌒

June 25, 1945

5 P.M.

Verviers, Belgium

Hello Sweetheart,

Herewith, regular mail service resumes.

We got here at 1 o'clock this P.M., having left Paris at 9 last evening. We had a wonderful time. We spent Saturday evening at a wonderful review, free to service men, sponsored by the French Liberation Committee, and then did a couple sidewalk cafes until midnight. Yesterday we took a grand tour of the city and saw all the famous places. I recognized a lot of them and some I didn't recognize at all. Les Invalides, the tomb of Napoleon, was so familiar to me. The Pantheon was unfamiliar (I had it all wrong in my mind), and when I saw the twin buildings of the Trocadero I was sure nothing like that belonged near the Eiffel Tower. I found out it was built in 1937. Even in Paris new things are built.

In the afternoon we did what all good Parisians do on a lovely Sunday afternoon. We went up the Tower (they allow you about a third of the way up) and then took a stroll down the Quai d'Orsay along the Seine embankment, crossed the river on the Alexandra III bridge, gaped at the exhibit of *Crimes Hitlerienne* in the Palais de Justice, then strolled on down the Champs Élysées, paid our respects at the tomb of the French unknown soldier, and walked back the Champs to the Place de la Concord and Tuilleries Gardens, pausing 2 or 3 times for a bit of liquid refreshment at our beloved sidewalk cafes. It was a typically Parisian way of spending a Sunday in Europe's most beautiful city.

My impression of the French is less favorable then it was 15 years ago. Their economic dilemma is a letter in itself, but the people somehow don't impress me. Five years of German occupation have weakened their self-reliance and initiative, more so by far than here in Belgium. They feel like martyrs and you get the impression that they want something for nothing. Whether it's a glass of wine or getting stripes sewn on a shirt, they've always got their hand out for a tip. That was always typical of France, but it seems grosser to me than before. This judgement, of course, is not well-considered, being based on so short a stay.

Nevertheless, Paris is beautiful, and I most certainly want to bring you over here to see it someday. I have mental notes of the top spots— I saw them all, except the Bal Tabarin and other cafes—going alone would make me feel bad. I'll let them gyp me there when you're along to join in the fun.

Now we're here at Jayhawk Rest Camp at Verviers and may be here several days. We've discovered the battery has left Fulda, and until we find out where they are we can't go back. So we'll see a few movies, go to the Red Cross, and enjoy Verviers on the government's time until they come after us. I do so want to be home. It's getting so nothing looks good to me anymore—lots of things are interesting but nothing is really fun. I wouldn't be surprised that you have something to do with that.

I imagine I'll have lots of mail from you when I get back. I'm surely looking forward to it.

My regards to everyone, love to the folks, and especially all my love for you, my darling, forever.

Always,

Your, Harold

⌐

June 28, 1945

Verviers, Belgium

Hello Dearest,

Still here at the Jayhawk Rest Camp. We don't know where the 219th has gone and they haven't gotten any reply to our wire to Johnny yet. It's quite a situation. We'll try to make the best of this soft life while it lasts. It's really too soft for me. However, in another few days, I'll be volunteering for something to do. For the moment I'm becoming a confirmed loafer.

I sent some postcards to you and a map of Paris. Also I mailed the lace centerpiece. Today when we go out I may find something else for you. Incidentally all the gifts from Paris were bought at the Galleries Lafayette (the Saks Fifth Avenue of the city), except the jewelry.

Last night we saw a stage show called *Section 8* put on by an Army troupe. Pretty fair, but after all the entertainment of the last week I'm getting a little bored—perhaps blasé is the word.

I see that the San Francisco Conference seems to have ended on an optimistic note. I'm quite sure it will be ratified by the Senate and from the looks of everything it should be generally accepted. I agree with Vandenberg that it's not perfect but I do think it's a start. Such an organization ten years ago, as the President said, would have prevented this war. But the world always has to learn the hard way—and the little guy pays for all of it. That's one reason why I'm still not too sorry why I'm serving in the ranks. This experience is giving me an appreciation of the average guy such as I could never have gotten elsewhere. I have nothing but praise for the little guy and the way he can take it. I'm proud to be among them.

This period now—following the halfway mark—is hard to go thru. Almost all of the men over here are homesick and all are sweating out furloughs at home or China-Burma-India. They are moving them out as quickly as possible but it will take a long time. Of course I haven't any idea about us in the last 10 days, but I do so want to come home. It's been nearly 8 months since I've seen you. My loneliness has become a part of me and will continue to be so. I fall asleep with you on my mind and wake up reluctantly dreaming of you. You needn't worry that I have built you up in my longing beyond the girl you are. I really see you as you are—and that's what I want now, as I have ever since that Memorial Day in 1937. My love for you during these months of separation and whatever is ahead has just gotten deeper inside of me. You motivate practically everything I do or am.

I don't feel futile writing all this to you from so far away because all we have to lick is time and what I feel for you is timeless.

Please be cheerful and hopeful—because that way you're irresistible.

I love you, my darling, always and with more love than I can express.

Ever,
Your, Harold

⤙

Gersfeld
July 2, 1945

My Darling,

Here we are at our new home. Colonel Roberts (a Harvard man) made a little speech of welcome. He told us we are scheduled for return to the States sometime between September 1st and Christmas. He feels "very confident" that we will not go to China-Burma-India direct. Also he "thinks" we are going to be operational or strategic reserve in the States, scheduled to ship if needed next year.

Now as to living quarters. We live in an exquisite baronial estate—

three to a room. We have hot water for the first time since leaving England. We have daily movies, a bar, library, and all the comforts of home. Some of the boys live in a hotel a block from here, but this modernized palace where a few of us live with the officers is the nuts. We even have cleaning women requisitioned from the village by the colonel!

The village of Gersfeld has a population about like Brunswick, Ohio—a tiny but very picturesque village dominated by this estate with one cobblestoned street. It boasts two swimming pools right on the estate and we have all the modern conveniences. We're 18 miles from Fulda, the nearest town of any size. We may not stay here until the Pacific-bound divisions precede us home. We shall wait in Germany doing very little until there is transportation available to bring us home—probably late in the year.

I think the big day's coming, honey. I'll be home for Christmas—1945.

All my love, darling—

> From your "ever-lovin,"
> Harold

∽

> 196 FA Gp
> APO 758
> Gersfeld
> July 3, 1945

Lo Darling,

Everything is very nice here except for the rain. It's beautiful country, but it rains everyday. We must be either down in a hole or up on a hill.

Last night Jerry Grimaldi and I went to the movies—saw *Rainbow Island*—what a crazy show! Tonight most of us are going back to the 219th at Fulda to spend the last evening with the boys. They leave tomorrow morning for LeHavre and an uncertain future.

For a long time I was rather restless, but now that I know I'm coming back to you fairly soon, I'm reasonably content. Keeping myself busy with reading, movies, my accounting, bull sessions, and work when there is any. I feel sorry for husbands who seem to have so little to look forward to that they run around enjoying their "freedom" whenever they are away from their wives. For me, being free means being with you. I don't believe that anyone is to be condemned on moral grounds under unnatural circumstances. The only girls I look at twice on the street are those who have some features resembling you—and none of them are half so pretty—in your way you're quite a gal.

The Jap homeland is certainly catching hell. It seems to me Japan's war potential will be completely destroyed long before she can be defeated in the field. When it comes to fooling with U.S. air power—that's murder. The Luftwaffe in its palmiest days was a pygmy by comparison. The destructive effect is awful—I know, I've seen plenty of results. And Japan power was never equal to Germany's and is fast dwindling. I see tremendous progress in the final knockout of this war in the next few months. And when we have China re-equipped and get 20 or 30 combat divisions from here furloughed and redeployed, you'll find they'll wish they had picked on someone their size. Japan's last hope of victory died when we crossed the Rhine. Alone she's a hard-to-get-at, hard fighting, second rate power faced with the resources and highly trained armies of two first rate powers—soon to be three I hope.

I just called Paris on the phone—business. Sounded as close as Fulda or Frankfort. Maybe I'll be able to call Wooster soon—I would be so thrilled I probably couldn't talk.

My love to the folks—

My heart to you—

Ever, Harold

My Darling,

Last night I celebrated Independence Day by reading the Memorial to President Roosevelt you sent me. It's wonderful. We are privileged to have "known" him—and what American didn't—the giant of our age.

We had a fireworks and rocket celebration here about 10 o'clock last night. Curfew for Germans is 9:30 but they made an exception so the Krauts could see how we celebrate the independence of God's country. Our Soviet comrades, 10 miles east of here, fired cannons to join the "Glorious 4th" celebration. If we were a little closer to the border I understand vodka was the "order of the day." The Russian border guards are in the new *Franklin Roosevelt Regiment*—first time the Red Army has ever honored a foreigner.

Well, the old gang has gone! Most of the boys came down to say goodbye but I was Sergeant of the Guard and couldn't go. I had said goodbye once. Joe and Terry were the only two real friends there.

I can now tell you this: We were located in Waltrap near Recklinghausen on the northern rim of the Ruhr pocket. We had three battalions of heavies shelling Dortmund 9 miles away. For us it was close—in fighting. There was a hell of a lot of shelling and I was on duty April 12 all night. We were firing on some German 88 batteries near the Ruhr River—a little creek that runs thru Dortmund and Essen. At about midnight Bill Phillips, our switchboard operator with the only outside connection, called me. He's a kid of 19, a fine boy, and very patriotic. He was crying a little and his voice broke. He said, "The Chief died today in Georgia." I was stunned. Of course it didn't seem possible and I thought he was putting on an act. The shelling we'd been giving them had been pretty heavy and I thought he was trying to relieve the tension. I said, "You're joking." Finally he convinced me and I guess I stared into space for ten minutes. Then I called the Colonel at the CP and told him. He just said, "God damn."

Later that night when the infantry heard it, several companies took no prisoners—alive. And the colonel ordered 100 sounds of heavy stuff earmarked for a salute if the war should end. It didn't end then so we never fired a salute. We did put out a flag at half mast the next day. The Kraut civilians all knew it by morning. I have never felt so alone— I guess we all did. That's how I got the news on the front. As I say, I couldn't tell you this then. The next night I was off and we had a rebroadcast of all the radio eulogies and music from the States. Even Colonel Fairchild broke down a little when Bing sang "Home on the Range." The Army loved FDR.

> All my love—
> Your, Harold

⌒

> July 9, 1945
> Gersfeld

Hello Darling,

I'm sure that recent letters have cleared the confusion about the transfer and our future probabilities. All speculating aside, the story as it now stands is that we will come home some time between Labor Day and Christmas—will have 30-day furloughs, and then be stationed at a post in the U.S. as part of the strategic reserve. If the war lags too long next year and they need us, we will go to the Pacific—if all goes well, we will not. Those are the War Department's present plans. More than that, not even the colonel knows.

Today the sun is shining brightly. The only trouble is that even a gorgeous day isn't much help without you. For the rest of my life, the period between the end of the war and the time I get back will be a great wait.

I'm sending today the pictures we took (Sam, Bernie, and I) at the Atrocity Camp near Paderborn. All the prisoners you see were Nazi war criminals and by now most of them have been executed, including the 300 women. Save these carefully. They are valuable to me.

We are all following the reports from the Pacific closely, and it seems as if everything is going as well as possible. There is every reason for confidence.

I highly approve of Jimmy Byrnes as Secretary of State. He'll do a bang-up job. He's definitely the best choice the President could have made. He's doing a good job of picking them all around. He'll never be another Roosevelt, but we could live to be 100 and we won't see a man the stature of F.D.R. But I like Truman—he's honest, conscientious, and has plenty of common sense.

By the way, take a look at the trash piles next time you go to Cleveland. We hear there is quite a stock of Norden bomb sites in our fair city—selling price 30 cents.

All my love, sweetheart, and a couple of million kisses just for today.

> I love you.
> *Ich du lebe.*
> *Je t'aime.*
> Your, Harold

> July 10, 1945
> Gersfeld

My Sweet,

I'm very happy you've decided to work steadily. Whether it is always convenient or not, it will keep you busy and I think the department you are going into is very interesting.

I've found a new hobby—or rather am indulging in an old one. I've started to play poker again. We play a 25 and 50 cents limit a couple of hours a night. It's 3 nights and I'm in $3. I'm not crazy about it but I've got to do something.

Yes, Liesl was broken-hearted when I left. She was so sad she didn't even show up to say "auf Wiedersehen." But I'm a rounder—I just met another one. She's got long blond pigtails and is all of about 2-1/2 years old. She lisps, and I can't quite understand her name. She's kind of mercenary though. She expects a stick of chewing gum before she'll play ball or even sit on my lap. She's very cute, although I don't entirely trust her. If anyone with 2 sticks of gum a day turns up, I'm sunk. Such is life without a wife—you've got to depend on the strictly gum digging variety of Kleine Frauleins. There's also a little girl about 5 living near here who is everybody's sweetheart. She's quite a little athlete (as are most German kids) and she has a rather harsh voice which has earned her the name of "Gravel Gertie." She's the little playmate of anyone and she can outrun us all—we're supposed to be in condition, but "Gravel" is really in shape. It's surprising how much fun kids are—they keep you human when you're inclined to "hole up" in loneliness.

I'm quite sure there's no phone service from here nor from Paris either. We're wondering whether we might see the President on his way to or from Berlin. For a few days the capital of the U.S. is nearer to me than to you—but that's slim consolation.

Don't worry too much about my little girl friend—she will take too long to grow up.

I love you, even if you don't have pigtails.

> Always,
> All my love.
> Your, Harold

⤳

Gersfeld
July 12, 1945

Lo Darling,

Our group was relieved from attachment to the 78th Infantry Division and is now attached to the 3rd Infantry Division. The 3rd is one of the occupation divisions. I'm quite sure it is just another temporary attachment while we cool our heels—the Army dotes on attachments for administrative purposes.

I think I've found a good laundress. She's a woman who does all my washing each week, including wools, for a bar of soap and a piece of candy. I just got the first one back—not bad work at all—of course she can't press clothes just right but it's all clean. She only lives a couple of blocks from here so it's an easy job to deliver it and pick it up. I'll be spoiled at prices for such services when I get home.

Well, I played poker again last night—was out 25 bucks at one time but ended up 25¢ winner. Tonight I think I'll lay off. I had to sweat to break even last night. I'm not much of a gambler. It's chief attraction is that it takes up time—and that's what I've plenty of.

We have a beautiful $4,000 grand piano here in the ballroom and I've been fooling around with it. If I spend much more time here I'll be pretty good at it. President Truman has the same hobby, I notice. I saw *Rhapsody in Blue* the other day so I'm trying to pick up some of the Gershwin tunes—but I wouldn't attempt the "Rhapsody" by ear.

We have such a beautiful place here that it's almost a shame to not be able to enjoy it—but I want to see the hills of home. It's funny how quickly time passed in combat and how it drags now. In combat we couldn't keep track of the days and nights (there was no night to sleep anyhow) and time just rolled around. But now—"time drags on with leaden feet."

Regards to the gang at the store.

With all my love—
Ever, Harold

↶

July 14-15, 1945
Gersfeld, Germany

Lo Darling,

Here is that long letter I promised you. In this group the CQ must stay up all night. It's only 9 p.m. now and I have 11 more hours to go.

At times I've gotten a little discouraged, but yesterday I visited a place that will make me ashamed to admit I've ever been blue. There is a DP camp near here containing about 6,000 people rescued from Buchenwald. Among them are 600 Jews, the remnant of over 50,000 who passed thru this camp during the Nazi regime. These 600, mostly late arrivals at Buchenwald, are the only survivors. They are all Polish Jews—there are hardly 600 Jews in all Germany that are pure German Jews.

We have been living pretty close to this place for some time now, but just heard of it yesterday, so Captain Lowenthal, Sam, Bernie Snyder, and I took off about 2 o'clock and went for a look-see. I won't ever forget it. The UB Army has them quartered very nicely in an x-casterine (German Army camp). The Jews have 3 large apartment buildings, probably German officers' living quarters previously. When we drove up they swarmed out of their buildings to greet us. Since all of us wear the map of Jerusalem on our faces we were literally overwhelmed. Most of them were men, but there was a smattering of women and children too. They don't look so bad as far as weight and general condition is concerned, since they've had two months of Army chow, medical treatment, and sun baths and rest since their release the first of May. But they bear testimony to their previous treatment in scars and various other more unmentionable indignities, women as well as men. The stories they told us in Yiddish, Polish, German, French, and English were almost impossible to believe. I won't go into detail about them now or probably ever. I found myself thanking God that our grandparents, yours and mine, were smart enough to leave this terrible continent. You can get down on your knees and thank heaven every night that you are an American. The minorities, and little people of Europe who were defenseless before this thing, are whipped. These people are getting their bodies restored but their minds are forever filmed over with the horrors with which they have passed. Out of 6,000,000 in Europe in 1933 there are now 300,000 left. I should have said Central Europe—that figure does not include those in England and Russia, at least the part of Russia invaded by the Germans at their high watermark in 1943. These people are destitute, homeless, frightened.

They don't want to go back to Poland where anti-semitism is as they say, a matter of the heart, while in Germany it flourished under orders. The U.S. government has promised them they needn't go back. They all want to go to Palestine but the British probably won't allow that. They are truly a people without a home. You can say all you want about the quality or lack of it of the Polish Jew—they may be poor, ignorant folk—but they are human beings and when they take your hand and look at you and say America—it is as though they were looking at a god whose status they could never hope to acquire. My heart was wrung. We gave them cigarettes and candy. These are Jews, and they were principally touched that we went to them to say hello. More we could not do. The questions that they ask: is there anti-Jewish feeling in America? Yah? But you don't have to step into the street when a Gentile walks by? Gut. Is President Truman as good a man as the great Roosevelt? Is he a friend of our people? Yah. Gut. And always—I have a sister, cousin, uncle, niece, in Brooklyn, Chicago, yes, even Cleveland and Toledo, Ohio. They talk about their life in Buchenwald as one would discuss hell if he had been there. They are worried about their future, about the present (you're not hard enough on the Germans—they'll fool you if you aren't careful), and in their eyes is the horror of the past. Yet, they are Jews and have not lost their sense of humor. They laugh readily if not heartily, they smile at our attempts to speak French, German, Yiddish. (I can't even attempt the latter.) We did remind them that we must still defeat Japan and they seemed to wish us well in that—"always troubles," one old geezer said in perfect Brooklyn English. Some of the girls were quite flirtatious, much to the annoyance of their boyfriends, and Bernie and I had our pictures taken by Captain Lowenthal with two of the "Buchenwald Belles." If it comes out I'll send you a copy—the only picture I've had taken with anyone else but you. But it was worth it—they were so happy to think we would pose with them. We are not smart, honey, we are just lucky, and don't you ever forget it. Now, more than ever before, the old snobbery is gone, and this time for good. There may be differences between various types of Jews, but the similarities don't allow for quibbling. From now on it's the person and not the background that counts. But there are deeper values. I won't repeat the things they told me about what they suffered, but they came sane out of a place we would have come out of as raving maniacs. Hitler did his work well. There will be no Jewish question in central Europe again in our lifetime—there are almost no Jews left to be the scapegoats in Europe. In the British Empire, America and Russia are the only Jewish communities left in the world. When I think of what was done to 5-1/2 million people because of their race and religion over here, my blood boils over. Whenever I get too big for my boots, I shall think of the 600 survivors of Buchenwald and it will make me very humble and very grateful.

I was going to tell you how anyone can get information about friends and relatives in Germany. Between us, the chances are 10-to-1 they're dead. Have them write to the U.S. Department of State giving full particulars. The next best bet is the Society of Friends—in other words the Quakers. There were 80 Jews out of 95,000 in the Cologne area left alive when we came in early in the year. About 40 more have returned. That's a good average of the percentage of German Jews left. There aren't any. The proportion of the French, Dutch, Belgian, and Danish Jews left is high because the people hid them. In Poland it was tragic.

So you baked a cherry pie? How about practicing on strawberry pies—I like them better. I guess the principle is the same. You surely were popular in Cleveland—you don't know how much good it does me to know you are preserving the normal balance of our lives and that you hold in trust the key to my return to civilian life.

I can't get that picnic out of my mind. You remember another Fourth of July at Mohican Park when I finally fell head over heels in love with you—that was 7 years ago. The feeling in that respect hasn't changed an iota. The very thought of you thrills me. I ordinarily don't go for picnics, but we are going to go on at least one when I come back—I've just got to get my arms around you in a secluded picnic spot—where you're concerned I'm still a wolf.

This is quite enough reading for you and writing for me. Be good, and keep that sweet chin right up.

Gratefully and with all my love,

Your, Harold

July 19, 1945
Gersfeld

Hello Darling,

Before going on guard last night I saw *Rhapsody in Blue* again. The music is so superb I couldn't resist it. Then I came home, sat down at "my grand," and worked out "The Man I Love" and "Embraceable You." Colonel Casale thinks I play well (he has no more ear for music than an ear of corn), and says he's going to try to get the piano tuned for me. That will be very nice.

We were all excited here over the news of the naval bombardment of the Japanese coast. Invasion can't be far off. Japan just isn't in the big leagues. Wild rumors are circulating here that Premier Stalin brought a peace offering from Japan to Pottsdam with him. Also that Russia is about to declare war on Japan. I don't believe either of them at the moment, but where there's smoke there's fire. I am starting to hope that Japan's industrial classes will gain enough favor with the Emperor to throw in the sponge before Japan is decimated. We have now reached the heart of the Empire. Perhaps Japan, like Germany, will have fought her hardest battles. It took 2 months to take Aachen—2 days to take Cologne, 2 hours to cross the Rhine. Okinawa took 82 days.

We can hope that Japan will come to her senses and surrender rather than be torn into a thousand bloody pieces as she will be as she continues her hopeless and unequal struggle. We've come far since Pearl Harbor.

I'll have to tell you a good one on myself. I took a pair of pants to a woman living near here to be shortened and explained what I wanted done—shortened 1 inch. "Ja, ja," she said. Today, just a few minutes ago, she brought them over. They are lengthened 1 inch. I had to call on the interpreter to help me out, and Captain Philbeck is standing here laughing his fool head off at my German. The poor woman just walked out with them shaking her head. In her book I'm a dummkopf. In mine—I no longer speak the language.

Are you still baking those delicious pies mother's been raving about? Or is being a working girl interfering with your cooking? Never mind about that. You're a good cook, and even if you weren't, I'd still be eating out of your hand.

With all my love,
Your, Harold

Gersfeld
July 23, 1945

Hello Darling,

As I am writing this letter and listening to a benefit performance from the Met, I am thinking that 6-1/2 years ago today was our wedding day. For the past 8-1/2 months, we've been apart physically. A long separation, forced on so many, affects them all. Our life has been based on perfect faith in each other.

No man could ask for more in a wife than I have in you. There is no more loyalty, devotion, and love to be had. You're not the "sweet" type and never were. I fell in love knowing that and I've never regretted it—"sweet" women aren't very interesting.

Six and a half years! It seems like yesterday. I think that's because I shall always see you as my bride. We never were "silly" about that at least in public. The only difference between us then and now is that all the living we've done has deepened our love. It's deepening even yet, at a greater rate, now that we must express it temporarily in ink instead of by action. That is what true love is, I think, sweetheart.

There came to me an analogy while thinking of all this last night. Love is like a young river flowing thru the hearts of those who will listen. The longer it flows, the deeper it cuts its way, as a river does thru rocks. Finally it creates a gorge, deep in the consciousness of the lovers, which time and space make only deeper. Silly, I guess, but that's the way I feel about it. Distance and time can only intensify it with an effect that will be lasting. I couldn't love you more than I do now.

I don't much believe in religion, but God has been very good to us. I know that the happy ending to this interlude of war in our lives is inevitable. May it come soon! When it does, I'll be with you to protect, and love and care for you—and to tease you a little too, my angel with a sense of humor instead of a halo. And when we get into our next house, I'm going to carry you over the threshold because I will have come back to you forever.

I love you, darling. Be happy.

Your, Harold

↩

Gersfeld
July 23, 1945

Lo Darling,

I'm sure you know by now that I won't be home quite as soon as I hoped. The men going home this year are those going for immediate shipment to China-Burma-India after furlough and a little training. The rest of us who are not Army of Occupation or scheduled for quick shipment to CBI will be among the troops coming home toward the end of redeployment. We don't know when that will be. You have every reason to feel relieved and happy—much more so than some whose husbands may be home first but won't be there too long before they're on their way again. I hope I didn't give you the impression I was practically on the boat. It could be six more months. Don't count days or months yet. The time element is completely uncertain. There's no reason to think I shall ever go to the Pacific, nor will I be indefinitely in Germany.

Now, about the 196th. I think I've told you all my friends except Terry and Joe are here. Casale could pick whom he wanted to take along and I went. It is a lucky break because the 219th boys are out at Le Havre sweating out direct shipment. This outfit is far luckier because most of these boys have been overseas for 18 months, and now we are getting the breaks.

I'm getting to know the fellows here pretty well and they're a swell gang. I don't like the Army but this is a good outfit to be with.

I am pretty sleepy but just wanted to talk to you before I kiss you goodnight and tumble into bed.

I love you, my adorable darling.

Forever Lovingly,
Your, Harold

Gersfeld
July 24, 1945

Hello Darling,

I admit I have tried to mention the desolation and ravages of war just sufficiently to impress you with my reaction to it, and from that point on, I've tried to see what I could without overdoing the stench of death—if I wanted to, I could make you pretty sick, but I came over here to protect you from that.

I usually observe things as I feel about them. It would be unbearably dull for me to start this way:

Dear Old Girl,

We've got diggings in the little village of Gersfeld, located 20 miles east of Fulda, in the province of Hesse. The town's activities are bound up with agriculture, for as you doubters know, the European farmer does not live in a farm house in the country but all farmers live in the village and walk, ride, or stagger to work. Gersfeld has a church, a schule, 2 barber shops, 1 butcher shop, 1 bakery, and 3 groceries

A railway station from which a train leaves for Fulda every morning and returns every evening. There are 25 or 30 houses plus the Schloss castle in which we live, in addition to 2 hotels. Before the Americans came, there were probably 500 people to 1000 in town, including refugees from bombed cities. It is so damned peaceful and quiet that you can hardly stand it. But the country life brings roses to the cheeks, old dear, and besides I get overseas pay.

Ta ta, Old Bean

Now that, in caricature, is a factual letter, about as inspiring as a Gideon Bible plus the Rotary Code of Ethics. I know it's the truth, but while I never lie intentionally, I do color the facts with my impressions. If I tried to chronicle a day, I'd be more bored writing it than you reading it. Since you are spared Gersfeld and the boredom of this life, I'd rather talk to you mostly with my mind rather than my eye. Some of the 85-point men are no better off than we are. After they've gone, the strategic reserve and dischargees go home so we should get home as soon as a lot of the dischargees. In August, almost all traffic will be China-Burma-India direct and the big shipments to the States will resume. It looks as if all space for the balance of the year will be for those troops now training for early combat in the Pacific. It will be any time from December until next spring until the rest of us can be accommodated.

Regards to all your fellow workers.

Ever, lovingly—
Your, Harold

Hello Darling,

I am practicing the piano now. I'm going into Fulda with the mail run to buy some sheet music—Strauss waltzes and some Schubert. I am going to start stagnating if I don't keep myself busy. You can't imagine how a normally energetic person like myself can so easily succumb to apathy if I don't watch myself. Most of the boys hate this monotonous life and take it all out in grumbling (the only word for it is the good old Anglo-Saxon and G.I. word: bitching).

When I get home for good, I want to be full of energy—because after that long vacation, you and I are going on to Texas and New York. I have got to get on the ball.

Tonight I was playing our songs—"Blue Orchid," "Deep Purple," "It Looks Like Rain In Wooster County Wayne"—down thru to our Army favorites—"Missed Our Saturday Night," "Got Too Much of Texas In My Soul," "Oh What a Wonderful Morning"—and the feeling when I do that is that you are with me. It helps so much to just sit there and bring you close with music.

Here's a good one on me. This morning I was sitting at my desk and our German housekeeper was sweeping the floor and mopping. I got up for a moment and when I sat down—no chair! Kerplunk on the floor. She thought I had gotten up for her to sweep there. Only 20 people saw it and I'm getting all kinds of unhelpful advise on how to sit properly. That happened to you once at the Southern Tavern when some jerk jerked it out from you. Results similar—hurt feelings. Does it ever make you feel like a fool? I've yet to be un-horsed, but I've sure been un-chaired. Who laughed the loudest?—Maria, the German housekeeper—that ingrate—and after I gave her a stick of gum two weeks ago, too!

Tis now the witching hour of 0015 (civilian 12:15 at night) and I better close this letter. I'm going to mention that picture in every letter until I get it—a good natural pose—it will be enough to keep me bewitched for the time when I have the original again.

I love you, sweetheart, every minute of the clock—so just resign yourself to that as a lifelong fate.

Always,
Your, Harold

August 1, 1945
Gersfeld

Lo Darling,

I imagine fall goods are coming in now and the back-to-school promotions are due to break. I was very interested in the personnel bulletin you sent from Dad. I agree very heartily with one article that states the greatest assets are store personnel. We, in the smaller stores who are active on the floor most of the time, should be the first to realize that. Too often we are inclined to put all our energy into correcting and none into praising. You will always catch more flies with sugar than vinegar. Employees of a store are not inmates of a penal institution, nor are they seminar candidates for Ph.D.s. They are people—like you and I—whose reactions will depend not on what you say to them but on how they feel about the way they are handled. Now that you've been at the store a month or so, I'm sure you know what I mean. If we would analyze our personnel policies as carefully as we analyze our merchandising, our store would run even better than it does now.

But enough of that. Tell Pop to keep on sending pertinent booklets—of course nothing he'd want returned. I shall be glad to get them. I'm starting, mentally, to prepare myself for civilian life.

The Japs are taking an ungodly pasting, aren't they? If you could count on them for a Western reaction you'd know the end was not far off, but they are unfathomable to our way of thinking and therefore we shall just have to keep on pouring it in. No country ever faced the prospects of so crushing a defeat as do the Nips. The clock has made a full round since that Sunday in December 1941.

What I'm really waiting for is the day I can hold you close and drink in the fragrance of your hair and the touch of your hand.

I love you.
Your, Harold

↩

August 3, 1945
Gersfeld

Hello Sweetheart,

I'm glad you liked the centerpiece from Belgium. By now I hope the things from Paris have arrived. I'm going to Frankfurt tomorrow and will try to pick something up for Mother. I don't really have any business there this time, but am going with Johnny Philbeck just for the ride!

No, darling, I don't think we'll insist on the Japanese having to give up their Emperor. What they must do, however, is surrender their Army—we can't make peace under any conditions that do not include the complete capitulation of that brutal force.

From what I read between the lines, politics isn't over your pretty head at all. You have a pretty sound idea of what's going on. Were I to go into politics, I should lean heavily on you as my severest critic—just as I do now depend on you for honest and common sense criticism. That ability is not usually lauded in the love songs, but no wife who can't do it is fulfilling her job. Anyhow, politics and war are all part of the same game.

As for your losing "an ounce," don't go on any crazy diets, please. I love you just as you are, liebling.

Meanwhile, to my adorable sales girl,
All my love and kisses,

Ever,
Your, Harold

↩

Gersfeld
August 6, 1945

Lo Dearest,

It is the witching hour of 5 A.M. so I am on guard tonight. The night has gone very fast, since Captain MacGregor, who is OD, and I have had a nice conversation. It ran all the way from horse racing to the Army and back to civilian life again—civilian life being what is on all of our minds.

The Potsdam Conference just ended has been notable, for what it didn't talk about as much as what it did. No mention was made of the Dardanelles and the relationship of Turkey and Russia in regard to this thorny question. Also the issue of Tangiers was not discussed. Then there is the very grave question of peace in the Balkans, a perennial, but still important to the settling of Europe. Japan was officially not mentioned but that is not surprising. Until and unless Russia officially declares war, no mention of the Far East is diplomatically possible.

In fact the only big problem that was reported upon as having been fully covered was Germany. I think it is a good settlement. Neither Britain, and certainly not ourselves, suffered anything like the sort of devastation and losses of population that Russian has. France was badly hit, but for much of her trouble she has her own untidy politics to thank, so she certainly couldn't be given anything like a proportional share of the spoils. It is unfair to some of the smaller countries whose heroic underground resistance made our task easier—such as the Netherlands, Belgium, Czechoslovakia, Yugoslavia, and Greece— but I believe their chief need is food and manpower. I'm quite sure that German labor will be available to them and for food they will have to depend this winter on United Nations Relief & Rehabilitation Adamination. This will be a very hard winter in Europe, and I believe one reason why so many non-occupation troops are being left here is to prevent rioting when hunger sets in. And it will set in all over the continent. If Europe had food, most of the problems with which she faces would solve themselves. This is the winter to watch—after next spring the worst danger will be over.

To get back to Potsdam, I am fully convinced that the most important decisions, aside from Germany, cannot be made public now due to security reasons. I still think Japan and the Far East were fully discussed and some decisions reached. I've given up hope that Japan will surrender, but I still think it is high time that her fate be decided. I am sure that Russia will make some contribution to the final defeat so that she may have a seat at the all-important peace conference on the Pacific.

It is too much to believe that it was entirely a coincidence that the unconditional surrender offer should be made while the President and Prime Minister were at Potsdam. Surely Joe was shown a draft and had some advice asked of him.

Europe is a boiling pot right now. Hunger can do strange things, and during this winter the good faith of those who stuck together to fight Hitlerism is going to be tested. If we don't feed them, there will be civil war in some of the freed countries. Only here in Germany will there be none. The Germans are licked and know it. The liberated countries will feel the grievance of famine if it comes to them. And they have strong leftist movement to take advantage of any hunger to press on their government's radical measures that will kill off any potential democracy of our Western type that is just trying to come to life. It is surely to our interest to protect the way of life here for which we have come so far to risk so much. A little less variety is a small price to pay for buying peace in our children's time.

By next spring the American Army will be largely cleared out of Europe except for the 400,000-man Army of Occupation. Also Europe's first post-war crop will be in, and in addition, the transport system will be functioning again and the worst will be over. But from November to April will be a period critical for the future of the world. The danger is Americans may not recognize it because there will be no American casualty lists over here.

I know you will take care of the folks' anniversary. By the way, I had forgotten, but I sent your folks a telegram for their anniversary in March and wonder if it was ever delivered.

Have you had the picture taken yet honey? I know you must have, but I want it so badly that I'm just going to keep on mentioning it.

This is a hell of a lonely life, isn't it? Not a single solitary God damn thing in this world makes much difference as long as we're apart and I'm not home with you and the family. I'm not trying to be a "good soldier," I don't give a damn about the Army, and I'm here because I have no choice. I'm so sick of the whole business that it includes everyone connected with it. Do I make it clear that I'm mentally a civilian again?

No mail for a couple of days. My love to everyone, and to you my darling, and with all my heart.

I love you.

Your, Harold

Gersfeld, Germany

August 21, 1945

6 P.M.

Hello Sweetheart,

Your V-J Day letter (unofficial V-J Day) was a mirror of my own feelings. It is such marvelous news that we can't help rejoicing even though our own reunion is not yet. We couldn't be so selfish to say that it means nothing to us that thousands of boys out there will come home.

I'm glad Al is coming back to the store. I know that will relieve Dad of a lot of pressure in the men's furnishings. It will be a pleasure to look forward to working with Al again.

I'm very glad you are not quitting work to help Mother. With the war plants starting to lay off a lot of surplus help, it can't be long until she gets someone, and I feel you need a steady job, now more than ever. The busier you keep now, the less time it's going to seem until I'm with you. In the last five days we've sent 6 men out of this group—all with 80 points or over and next week we expect to lose 12 more 75ers and up, and so it goes. All point scores are still based on V-E Day. I count my military service, from the personal point of view, from November 7th last year. It wouldn't be fair to look at it any other way. The men who were fighting thru northern France and Italy which we were living off the post are entitled to priority now. I don't think there's any doubt about that. And in spite of all the wild rumors both pro and con (rumors are as important to an Army as ammunition), I still think with my measly little 44 points, I'll be home this coming spring. A funny world, isn't it? Just when you stop worrying about civilian points, you start worrying about military points.

Oh, about that salami. I just didn't like the looks of it and one of the boys from Brooklyn (where the tree grows) said he'd eat it, and by heavens he did—in one sitting without bread. It takes all kinds of people.

The 69th Division is leaving for home! Some of our boys joined it today.

I like your answer to my question about what you're being paid. It shows I wasn't such a fool persuading you to marry me. An answer like that shows love, common-sense, loyalty, a sense of humor—and an appreciation of 50 cents an hour. Seriously, even though I've said it before, you're tops.

All my love to you, Rosebud.

Ever,
Your, Harold

Gersfeld, Germany
August 23, 1945
10 P.M.

Sweetheart Darling,

I don't think I've ever discussed the very colorful practice the Army has of using code names. Every outfit has a code name. For instance, the 219th received the code name of Casino as soon as we arrived in England and will carry it until it arrives back in the States. The 196th has the very suggestive name of Lustful. Our battalions are Cigar, Highcard, Circus, Coastal, and Jealous. Tonight the telephone to the 957th was out and when I couldn't reach them direct, I asked the operator at Fulda Switch—How can I get Jealous—after which we all had a big laugh. There are some screwy names all right—the 479th Tank Destroyer BN. is named Snooks. There is a Cleveland, Cleaver, Murder, Angel, Torrid, Frigid, Mississippi, to mention a few of the more colorful. We had quite a time understanding why the Germans laughed at our code name Casino when we came into combat. The advance detail used to go out and mark buildings at our next firing position. "Reserved for Casino" and often when we would move in we would be greeted with puzzled but smirking expressions from the populace. Then we found out that in Germany a Casino is a high class whorehouse. But it's the name the Army gave us, so we had to use it. We probably disappointed some of the natives when the battery moved in sans women to give the name its German meaning. There are laughs in war too. One girl even came up to Colonel Casale once and asked him in halting English whether he needed another girl for his brothel. You see, the German Army had regular traveling brothels for their troops and the mistake was natural, but very embarrassing.

I saw another cute movie tonight—Judy Garland and Robert Walker in *The Clock*. Their parting at the end reminded me of the last place I saw you—at about 3 o'clock on the afternoon of November 7 driving up the ramp of the garage at the Netherlands. I shall never again have such a black moment, for now we are waiting out what we once worried out.

Depending on whether Congress is going to be fair or not, or whether they will have courage and decency to draft men to replace lower point men quickly, we will be together soon. I still have enough faith in the American sense of fair play to be sure they will replace us.

I shall say goodnight, darling. Take care of yourself, and keep your sunny disposition. I love you, sweetheart, and my real life now consists of daydreams of our future together.

With all my heart, Ever,
Your, Harold

〰

August 23, 1945

Hello Sweetheart,

I have suffered my first wound. I have an ingrown hair where I sit down, and it was so darned uncomfortable, I had to go to the dispensary. I have a cute little bandage there now. I just knew I couldn't get out of this without an injury.

Points, points, points—that's all you hear around here. I feel very "unveteranish" around these 70 and even 60 point men!

Your work seems to interest you a lot. I hope you continue to enjoy it.

Things are getting pretty dull. We make up all kinds of rumors. Grimaldi is now working in the office and is shamelessly looking over my shoulder at every word I write. And Sergeant Thompson (of Springfield, Ohio) is bothering me with "reports" that the point score has dropped. Sam just walked in and sends his love. Grand Central Station.

Well, my friends are getting me so mixed up I'll have to suspend operations. Thompson says the score is jumping. So am I. These guys apparently aren't interested in me writing to you today, so I guess I'll have to give up. I'll write you again later in the day when Grimaldi and his ilk are out of the way.

All my love, darling.

Ever and always,
Your, Harold

〰

August 24, 1945

Hello Sweetheart,

This outfit is being transferred to a category IV. That means inactivation. I hope they'll take us all to the states with them. I'm glad to see the War Department is catching hell on all sides for its policy on medium-point men. The occupation forces can be very small and do the job. It's just a lot of malarkey, and selfishness on the part of the higher-ups, to try to retain men who have seen combat. I hope they don't get away with it. I also hope that our allies in the Pacific will be asked to share the occupation of Japan. With the furor now being raised, I think the War Department will be forced to lower its manpower sights.

I am really getting sick of the Army, honey. I can't remember ever being more anxious for anything in my life than to get out of this accursed country and come home. That 2nd honeymoon looks better and closer. Plan it just the way you want it—that is exactly what I want. To be with you day and night, to hear you laugh, watch your smile, touch your hair, and hold you while we dance. To know that it will be not only for the honeymoon, but for always—with never a fear of a separation longer than a hurry trip to the market.

I've gotten quite philosophical. I know now what some people waste their lives looking for. I know what is my happiness. It is you, always with me.

> I love you.
> Ever,
> Your, Harold

Gersfeld, Germany
August 28, 1945

Lo Darling,

We think we know where we are going. The colonel from the 79th
F.A. Group was here today and says he is left with only 30 men in his
outfit and wants all of us who have less than 55 points. That means
Babbitt, Yates, Humason, Price, Winter, Williams, Phillips,
Pietrusewicz, and me. Also, Grimaldi and Snyder—in other words, the
whole 219th gang. It will be a swell deal for the few months we have
remaining in the Army to get with the 79th Group. It is the oldest F.A.
Group in the Army and known as one of the nicest. It is located in
Marburg, about halfway between Fulda and Kassel—about 65 miles
from here. Marburg is the 15th largest city in Germany and one of the
least damaged, so we should be able to get decent quarters for whatever part of the winter we spend here. I shall be glad to get back to a city
atmosphere after two months in this tiny hill village, although we've
been quite comfortable. I met the colonel and he seems very decent.
We are losing all but four of our officers. The only officer from the
219th who will come with us is Lieutenant Aranoff from Dallas, Texas,
who joined us in combat. We are fervently hoping that Seventh Army
approves our transfer en masse because at this late date, we want to
stick together. For the matter of months we still have in the Army, why
not be among friends. Yes, we are hopeful about the 79th as our last
Army outfit, and it will remove the fear that we might have to sweat
out a boat while among strangers. I shall let you know as quickly as
possible about the transfer when it comes. I'm sorry I can't tell you to
stop writing yet, but I would be without mail for the rest of the year if
you did.

Remember I wrote you that Sam, Bernie, Captain Lowenthal, and I
went out to see some Jewish survivors of Buchenwald about six weeks
ago. Bernie and I were persuaded by Captain Lowenthal to have our
pictures taken with two of the women. These two women, bad as they

look, are Polish Jews who survived over 5 years in concentration camp. They got quite a kick out of the pictures, and Captain Lowenthal who has been giving them dental service took prints to each of them. It's a shame to think that human beings should be treated like that. But the Germans are going to keep right on paying for what they did. I shall be around here to help Ike preserve the peace and teach them a lesson.

I'll bet it's a thrill to say "fill 'er up." We'll be saying that on the way to Texas next spring, won't we, honey? And you just stick to chocolate "sodys" until I can get you back to the Balinese Room.

I know the worst is over, and when I do come home, we shall be together forever.

I'm glad to see that Bobby Feller is back with the Cleveland Indians. I hope that trend continues so that when I arrive home, it will be normal. I am going to be the most peaceful, civilian-loving citizen you ever saw. All I want is you and everything we enjoy.

With all my love, darling.

Ever,

Your, Harold

ᔐ

Gersfeld

August 29, 1945

Hello Honey,

Guard comes around so often that I seem to meet myself most of the time since we've lost so many high-pointers. However, it's about the only thing we get very often, so I can't complain.

Have you ever heard anything in your life to compare with the stream of rumors about shipments home and critical scores? It's almost funny—every official and general propounds his own plan. One day it looks like I'll be out in a month and the next it looks like a lifetime job. They certainly intend to use plenty of troops in occupation—400,000 here and 800,000 in Japan according to the President. With all other forces that are required, that means a 2,000,000 man

Army for at least a couple of years. Regular Army and new draftees will account for only 800,000, so that leaves 1,200,000 to be veterans.

There is really lots of interesting news. The report on Pearl Harbor released today startled all of us with the implication that General Marshall might have been partly responsible for the tragedy of unpreparedness that struck us on December 7th, 1941. I sincerely hope not, since George Marshall has done a wonderful job in my opinion and is surely one of the outstanding Chiefs of Staff.

Then there's the exciting story of our gradual entry into Tokyo Bay and the occupation to take place within a few days. It is thrilling to think of our great fleet, proudly flying the Star and Stripes, moved into the heart of Japan's power to accept an unconditional surrender.

We in the ETO will soon provide news of our own. The war crime trials will start in Nuremberg in a few days. I don't think the rats have a chance of getting off.

Like all couples who yearn for a reunion, the war will be over only when they let us come together again. As long as they continue the draft, we can be confident it can't be more than months away. All I ask is fair consideration when they get the high-point men out that they don't stop but keep right on. I wouldn't be surprised if they discontinued the point system by the first of the year in favor of discharge. I'm quite sure that any man with 3 years honorable service won't have long to wait—I am in my 33rd month.

Since I'm on duty, I brought Levant's book out here with me and perhaps I can attain *A Smattering Of Ignorance* before I am off duty.

I love you and always will, and that fact is as unchanging as the earth on which you stand. Yes, I love you, darling, sweetheart and I miss you like almighty hell.

Ever,
Your, Harold

Lo Darling,

We were very pleased to learn tonight that we shall get credit for both general and overseas service time from V-E to V-J Day. I will have 51 points. I'm glad to get over the 50 mark because it looks as though they are going to send home first all those with 60 points or more. Perhaps I'll get out on age before I do on points. The figures released by the WD about size of occupation forces are somewhat higher than I thought they would be, but I can't see why it isn't possible to fill them from men who are still at home and have never left. As to the more immediate question, and less important one, of where we are going from here—we don't know a thing. I still think it may be the 79th FA Group.

How's my working girl? Are sales holding up pretty well? By now, school business should be started. Have you any nylons yet? I'll bet it's wonderful to look forward to having all the things you had to do without. According to the information we read about the production of cars, it should be several months before it will be possible to get a new car. But everything in its proper place—stockings, radios, husbands, and cars in that order. I'm really very optimistic now.

From all reports, the Japs are behaving themselves pretty well. The showdown will be when Mac lands. I personally don't think there'll be much opposition. Japan is beaten badly, and when she's gone this far in her plans to surrender, it would be impossible for her to back out. I don't trust them, but I don't think they have the luxury of a choice. There will undoubtedly be a few more hari-karis.

When you get this, it will be Rosh Hashanah. Happy New Year! Next year we'll spend the holidays together. This year we can thank God that this terrible war is over. I shall go to temple myself, for that very purpose. I don't think I'm any more religious than I was before but I will feel closer to you and home if I observe that day.

Don't let them overwork you, sweetheart, and take good care of yourself—you belong to me.

With all my love, always,
Harold

❦

Hello Sweetheart,

I don't really know what they're thinking in the United States about how this job is going. We are going to allow the German people a lot of self government as early as next year, and we are making them all work like hell now to lay up food and fuel for this winter. Ike says we shall have to import some food for them. If it must be done, it must. You can't build democracy by emptying people's stomachs. But we are not naive. They shall not prepare for war again. The great trusts of iron and steel and chemicals which have been Germany's standbys have been dismantled and German heavy industry, only 25% destroyed, is being given to other countries or systematically destroyed. No, they'll not rise again to make war. But they will rise again. Our Republic is founded on the principal that all men are created equal and that we must secure liberty and justice for all. We know now that if we are to live our lives out in peace we must insure that to all people. That is the job of all of us—with malice toward none but the perpetrators. You'll never put a people down by force—only by justice and kindness can you triumph. In the few months I have to spend here yet, I'm going to expect to see the beginnings of a new Germany arise from the hearts of this people. Only in that hope can the world be secure. We must help them. It will be hard for them, and should be, but for our own future it must be done. No silly pampering—and no charity—but justice.

I'd better get to bed now—to dream of you, I hope, and how glorious it will be when I am with you again.

With all my love—Ever,
Your, Harold

❦

Lo Darling,

Things are happening pretty fast. We just got a phone call from Corps that the 196th Group (taking only enlisted men over 60 points and officers over 85) is leaving Tuesday the 11th for Camp Cleveland at Rheims, France, on the first leg of their trip home. Those of us who aren't going to be able to make it, as the Colonel puts it, are probably due to be transferred out Sunday or Monday to God knows what outfit. I imagine I'll go to a class I (occupation) outfit at least at first until the Army gives us V-J points and decides whether my 51 are enough to get me from an occupation unit to a class II outfit which will get me home more quickly. At the moment all is confusion in the Army and one gets the impression that V-J Day caught the Army woefully short of plans for demobilization. Even though I seem to be one point short at the moment, I believe it will take them a couple of months to make final decisions on how many and precisely who is to stay for the occupation. The period from the first rumors of Jap surrender until at least October will always be to me the "Age of Confusion." I'm determined not to worry, and enjoy what I can of this beautiful German September. There's plenty of time to worry about when they're going to give me a break. There are still 1,000,000 men overseas with over 18 months service. When they get home I'll have 12 months in myself and will start to get excited.

My cold has left me and I'm feeling fine. I hadn't been out of Gersfeld for a month so last night I went into Fulda to a movie. Saw *Roughly Speaking* with Rosalind Russell and Jack Carson. With all this excitement going on I find accounting work a little boring just for the moment so I started to read again. Finished some short stories by Saki and another small book of stories written by Thomas Mann. Today I've started *The Seventh Cross*, by Ann Seghers. It's a story of escape from the Gestapo. I have had the pleasure in recent months of meeting some of the arrogant bastards who make up that very interesting organization and I am enjoying Miss Seghers' book because the characterization of these people is so perfect. If I do have to spend some months in MG work, I should like to do intelligence work with prisoners. With a trusted interpreter I should be able to keep pretty interested. All of the Nazi's aren't captured yet by any means. In fact I think sometimes that most of them aren't. Most of the people of this country, as any country, are harmless, but they had a strong leaven of Nazi's and fanatics all throughout Germany. Right here in Gersfeld the day before yesterday they picked up Gauleiter of the Anti-Jewish-Society of Belgium—in other words the Julius Streicher of Belgium who had come here to hide out. In fact the man who delivered him to the Belgian police of Frankfurt is a chap you know—Jackie Perron. Jackie, usually so good-natured and smiling with his "disses" and "dats" rode in the back of a jeep all the way to Frankfort beside this rat with a pistol in his ribs. It was loaded. I can't imagine Jack doing this but he thought of all his Jewish friends and it made him mad to think of a guy like that having any comfort so he made him get on his knees in the jeep for an hour and a half. When they got there the guy couldn't even stand up so he kicked him out of the jeep and the Belgian gendarmes took him from there. Imagine finding a top war criminal in Gersfeld—a town of only 500 people. And so it goes—the hunters are now the hunted. Tonight the Jews of Germany, what are left of them, are celebrating the New Year in synagogues and meeting halls of Hitler Jugend. The Military Government has ordered all the Burgomeisters to make facilities for their services available to them. The worm has turned. Many of them are going to have to depend on Army chaplains or rabbis since there are almost no rabbis extant in this country. But for the first time since 1932 the Jews of Germany will hear the sound of the Shofar tonight—thanks to the United Nations.

It could be that we'll be moved out of here within 24 hours. I may make more changes from now on than I've made since I left for Fort Hayes in January of '43. Some of the letters may be lost. Don't send any packages.

When I get to my new outfit I may get a line on something for the future. Meanwhile, be good and don't worry. I'll be seeing you, in plenty of time to get started on that "A" project of ours—namely a family. One question—do you think she'd look cute in pigtails?

Ever,
Your, Harold

~

September 10, 1945
10 P.M.

Lo Sweetheart,

Here I am, assigned to 3rd Infantry Division in a pleasant little town whose name I don't know yet. I had thought several of us would be together, but after we got here this P.M., they really put the knife to us. Pietrusewicz, Winter, Williams, Phillips, Humason, Grimaldi, and Snyder were all scattered to the four winds. Only Yates and I were retained in headquarters.

We are living, for the first time since leaving Shelby, in Army barracks. This place, about 12 miles south of Kassel, is a former HQ for a German railway battalion. These are nice barracks with individual rooms and it's going to be OK. I am staying here because they didn't have a Message Central Chief—so that's me. It isn't exactly a castle, but it's adequate and I shall make out very well. Lieutenant Aranoff is here and he's been swell. The old 219th is now gone with the wind.

This was a move of about 68 miles. We had a pleasant trip and although Yates is rather lonesome for the gang, I feel rather good. After all, nothing is permanent in the Army. And here I'm really a high point man. Everybody seems to think I'll be home by the first of the year.

I'll write much more tomorrow, dearest.

Love to all. Pleasant dreams.

Ever,
Your, Harold

~

September 11, 1945
9:30 P.M.
Melsungen, Germany

My Darling,

The first day has passed here and I know the name of the town. I've had a bath and have patches put on my clothes (3rd Division Patch—lined part blue, rest white), gotten a little acquainted at Message Center, and generally I'm getting along OK.

My principle concern at the moment is my mail. I sent out forwarding cards to every forwarding APO in sight but still expect to go two weeks without any.

Joe Atlas, my message center clerk here, is from New York and went to Ohio State for one year. He knows Sammy Shapiro. He and forty other guys here are from 69th Division and were sent to this outfit when the 69th left.

I like it quite well here, although I hope not to stay very many months. I am really a high point man too. It's a relief to get away from these high pointers. Now 44 is something they're envious of!

I'm surely glad I'm a Staff Sergeant. The 3rd division is regular Army and everything is for the officers and first three graders. I pull no guard, no CQ, no nothing but my own job. And we have German orderlies who clean our quarters for us—just like the officers. Oh, the Regular Army is OK if you have enough rank and no brains.

I'm going to town tonight and will write you all about Melsungen. Poor Yates with his two stripes is suffering from an inferiority complex and loneliness. I have neither and am going to try to make it as easy as possible for him.

With all my love—
Ever, Harold

Melsungen, Germany
September 12, 1945

Lo Darling,

My morale, which was going up pretty fast in view of all the optimistic things I've been hearing, took a new slump to an all-time low
today when we heard via radio and the Stars and Stripes the point
breakdown. This is all V-J scores—mine is 52. It seems likely that most
of the men having less than 60 points will have to be retained a number of months, dependent upon how quickly reinforcements arrive.
That number will take into account the Army of Occupation and the
cleaning up force of 300,000 which will be here in this theatre up to 6
months. That means I will be in this group not going home this year.
It does not give any definite assurance of when I will go.

These Congressmen are running in circles, each racing the other
for any scheme that will pull votes. It's like a slot machine—I may
accidentally be benefited or not. If replacements are slow, I may not be
home until summer. The War Department, as usual, is in no hurry to
demobilize. The longer they keep a big Army, the larger their appro-
priations will be and the longer the regular Army officers will keep
their higher rank. We, the citizen soldiers, are the victims, and
Congress thru its wrangling is playing right into the Army's hands. It
isn't fatal or terrible, but the prospect of spending extra months is not
pleasant.

But, one way or the other, I love you with all my heart always—
near or far.

Ever,
Your, Harold

September 14, 1945
Melsungen, Germany

Hello Sweetheart,

I haven't told you much about where I am now so here goes: Melsungen is a city of 5,000 people located 12 miles south of Kassel. It is an average German town, picturesque and poor. War never hit this area. This part of Germany was cut off by the historic pincers movement of the 2nd armed and 3rd armed divisions driving from north and south to meet east of Kassel. The Krauts trapped in this pocket just gave up.

Even though this town is larger than Gersfeld, it doesn't have much to offer. There is a G.I. movie, a beer hall, and das ist alles. Fratting is more widespread in this town than any I've ever been in. The guys take girls to the movies and the beer hall and the two local inns are said to do a land office "honeymoon" business over weekends. There are going to be some explosions one of these days because the Germans are coming home in increasing numbers and are amazed at how much the local yokelry prefers the Americans. One fraulein told Bernie Snyder back in Gersfeld that she likes Americans because they are not so serious and thrifty (stingy) as the Germans were even when they were winning. And besides the German have no zigaretten, cow-gummi, and shokalade to give them. All I know is everybody in Europe now says "OK." That's one Americanism that has reached around the world.

I believe I wrote you that we are living in a German *caserne* (camp). It is quite comfortable—and we have all the modern conveniences except hot water. The bath house we use is the public one in town. I am used to just 3 a week so that's OK with me. On the whole, we live fairly well. The mess is good—far better than the 196th where it was really pretty bad. Just simple Army fare, but nourishing.

I'm trying to work a deal to get our mail from Fulda APO before they send it to the distribution center.

My clerk is a Jewish boy from New York named Joe Atlas. He's a very nice fellow and really knows his stuff. I haven't found a thing in this office that needs reorganizing. We handle a hell of a lot of traffic here so it isn't as dull as in a small group. Some of our battalions are so far away that they contact us by plane.

The situation in the Balkans is rather touchy. The London diplomatic meeting is going to have some rough going. King Peter of Yugoslavia is obviously trying to get the Western allies to back him against Russian-backed Tito. That's why the Moscow ambassadors of the U.S., Britain, and France have been called to London. If they tell the story, I believe that will leave the King without much support. I don't think anyone is ready at this time to quarrel with Russia.

There seems to be considerable criticism of MacArthur's treatment of Japan. After all, we did agree to a military occupation but with a Japanese civilian government. Under those circumstances it is impossible to move as quickly in extirpating militarism there as it would be otherwise. But it is a very delicate job and there's no use acting tough until the undefeated Jap Army has laid down their arms. Any other course would invite unnecessary bloodshed.

There's one thing about our occupation here that I don't understand. We have acquired an unhealthy respect for German property. It goes so far as to be ridiculous. When, for example, an officer I know found out that a couple of bedroom chairs in a hotel occupied by troops were accidentally broken, he had them fixed for the German hotel owner at government expense. In my opinion that is contrary to the spirit of a victorious army. The burden of support of such an army must be on the defeated peoples, and there's no use pretending you're a welcome guest when in reality you're an unwelcome intruder.

I've been so busy getting settled here in my job that I haven't had time to study. I'm getting settled now and shall soon be able to knock out the remaining chapters in my mercantile accounting course.

After supper I'm going to write to the folks. I can't wait to get home and know that I can cherish you and keep you near me as long as we live.

With all my heart.
Your, Harold

~

Gersfeld, Germany
Labor Day 1945

Lo Darling,

The war must be over—Labor Day was a holiday even in the Army this year. I remember that Labor Day exactly 6 years ago when we were riding to Youngstown and heard His Majesty speak from London and Premier Daladier from Paris. Six years, less one day, later it was all over. A long, bitter six years, but it preserved the civilization of the world for our lifetime and I hope for our descendents.

I had a nice Labor Day. I slept all morning and sun bathed all afternoon. I have a slight cold which I hope the sun will have taken care of.

Still no order for us. They're going to come—no doubt about it—but so far they just haven't. No move will mean much to me until it's headed for home. One place over here is the same as any other.

Well, in order to humor my cold, I'm going to turn in for a good 8 hours. Be good, darling, and pleasant dreams—of me I hope.

With all my love,
Ever,
Your, Harold

~

September 15, 1945
Melsungen, Germany

Lo Dearest,

I'm sitting in the Message Center this bright afternoon listening to Lohengrin coming from the Met 5,000 miles away. It sounds beautiful.

I'm afraid I won't be able to attend services on Yom Kippur. Of course I could go, but Joe is Orthodox and since there are just two of us I'm going to let him go. What religion I have isn't very closely tied to ceremonies. It would be slightly sacrilegious to sit all thru the solemn service just praying for my boat. So, as I did on New Year's, I shall read my service right here.

This surely is a busy office. I've been interrupted three times. Sometimes the way the phones ring and generals call up here you'd think I was running traffic for the whole Army. That part I like, but only because it makes the time pass more quickly.

This 3rd division is some outfit. It landed on the beaches before Casablanca in August of '42 and has been here ever since. Of course very few of the men who were with it then are still around. Most are home, lots are dead. The 3rd was activated in 1898 for the Spanish-American War and has been a going concern ever since, being one of the 9 divisions in our small peace-time regular Army.

Another interruption—a long one this time. I'll have to quit or miss the evening mail run honey.

With all my heart darling and for all my life.

Ever,
Your, Harold

September 17, 1945
Melsungen

Lo Sweet,

I've been busy as hell all day. We've got an officer (gentleman by act of Congress) called Gooch—that's his name. His rank is Lt. Colonel. His temper is ferocious and he checked his brains at the POE before he came overseas. He's not supposed to have anything to do with my section but today he came in and requested we change our methods of doing things. He was very polite about it, but I believe he's just another Casale. Well, I was polite too, of course. I couldn't very well be otherwise—in an argument I couldn't win—but I anticipate trouble. I remember him from 69th days—he was CO of the 724th FA at 2nd Avenue and 60th Streets and had a bad reputation. So tomorrow I'm going to division at Bad Wildungen and set a control system of my own if I can. The best way to get around these difficult officers is to go way ahead of them—I'll have Gooch's eyes popping in about two days—he'll either give me the bronze star or he'll bust me. Probably however he'll do neither—just pretend it was his idea all along.

The radio seems full of talk that they are thinking of discharging all men with two years service. I hope so—even three would be OK, because I'll never get transportation before Christmas anyhow.

Well, Yom Kippur is over—and I let it pass. I don't mind—these holidays are just something to get past until we can enjoy them together.

Honey, if they are available, would you send me a box of Hershey's with almonds? I understand they can be gotten by writing direct to Hershey, Pennsylvania, and they mail them. We get candy but it's lousy. Thanks.

I can't think of anything more tonight. I'm tired and think I'll take a little walk and go to bed.

Keep smiling, and wishing. With all my love.

Ever,

Your, Harold

⌇

Hello Lover,

There is a rumor around that 3rd division artillery is moving near Frankfurt in a couple of weeks to better quarters for cold weather. Since I expect to spend the coldest part of winter on this side of the pond, I shall be glad to move to something a little snugger than German Army barracks which are OK in nice weather but will be a little chilly this winter.

Speaking of being here, I am very happy at General MacArthur's announcement that 6 months from now only 200,000 troops will be needed in Japan. That is bound to have quite an effect on the grandiose schemes that WD politicians in Washington have cooked up for this theatre.

I'm enclosing some pictures taken Labor Day weekend in Gersfeld. You can see I spent as typically American Labor Day as possible—with pool and all. The estate was "loaned" to the Army by Baron von Wildhausen. Quite a joint too.

The radio just played "These Foolish Things," "Don't Get Around Much Anymore," and "That Old Feeling." They're breaking my heart. God, I'm lonely—but strangely enough I'm not unhappy. As a matter of fact I feel pretty good. I have gotten used to this feeling of tension that is always present. In spite of the fact that morale seems to have sunk to a new low around here, and all over the Army for that matter, mine is holding up very well. One thing that's helping it is Joe Atlas. You'd like him—and will when you meet him. He, along with Sam, is one of the few Army people I have any desire to see after this thing is over.

Well, I haven't had a letter from you since August 30.

And as the radio swings into "Deep Purple," here's all my love darling, forever, and a day.

> I love you—Ardently,
> Your, Harold

P.S. Yates is the only "survivor" of the 219th still with me.

〜

Melsungen
September 19, 1945

Lo Dearest,

The mail orderly made me very happy today when he brought me four forwarded letters—two from you, and one each from Mom and Pop.

I'm sorry I disappointed you by telling you it would probably be April until I get home. I must confess I did it deliberately. I knew everyone at home would expect the war to end on Sunday and have all the boys home by Thursday noon. It just can't work that way. I wanted to protect you from false optimism. As you read of the confusion resulting from the sudden end of the war, perhaps you'll understand better, darling, that I knew about where I stood in the mobilization. As I've explained I had no right to expect any further action this year, and believe I'll be among the high point men in AO to be relieved early.

It's going to be OK. Don't worry please. I remember how despairing you were in the early days of Hitler's triumph. I think I told you then we would win. In the long run I'm usually right. The main thing we have to do is not ever let this get us down although I admit I feel low plenty of times. But we're still in this thing although on the home stretch, thank God.

I understand perfectly when you miss writing for a day or two. You just write as often as you feel like darling, and I'll understand. I only want you to promise me not to ever despair.

On the Japan thing—not a chance. When I do come home I'll stay! We have just found out that we are moving in a couple of weeks to Darmstadt south of Frankfurt. The quarters will be better. No change of mail.

Nothing new here, dear. I appreciated one of Dad's rare letters very much. Keep busy, and make the days and weeks roll instead of drag.

With all my heart—to the most wonderful girl in the world. (How did I ever get you?)

I love you.
Ever, Harold

⌣

My Darling,

I got four or five Daily Records today and a bundle of trade journals. I was sorry to notice that Coach Boles died. He knew his job thoroughly and has been indirectly responsible for many good times I enjoyed at the Wooster stadium.

V-J points are now official. I have 51 points. The Army of Occupation is set at 55 points and down. On every count, I am ready and waiting for the next break in age, points, or service. One thing that is going to delay a lot of us middle pointers who just made the AO is that 12 or 14 divisions full of low point men were sent home before V-J Day to be redeployed to the Pacific. Most of those men will not be needed there and will eventually be sent back here. I shall start to get excited when 1946 comes—for the balance of this year I don't expect miracles—and I know '46 will see me home. That's when we should start to get impatient.

I have been very interested in the Conference of Foreign Ministers going on in London. We have already set up a bloc of Western powers to oppose the Soviet bloc. Great Britain, France, and ourselves seem to be "sponsoring" Italy and Greece, while Russia is "sponsoring" Poland, Bulgaria, Rumania, and Yugoslavia. This is the first step toward the possibility of future misunderstandings in Europe. I know from personal experience during my six months in Germany how anxious the Germans are to split Russia from her Western allies. How tragic it would be if reactionaries at home and in England and Russia provoke hard feelings at this critical time. What the present situation calls for is mutual trust. Up until now we've all been too suspicious of one another. Unless we want to prepare a war for our children, we've got to set this "power politics" business aside forever and try to make what we started at San Francisco a living thing. What has happened here since the war has half-killed it already. I don't regret my service, nor the remaining months I must spend in uniform, but for God's sake let's try to learn the lesson this time.

German local elections have been set in our zone for January by General Eisenhower. If these are successful they will lead to a larger measure of self-government for the Germans. I believe the British have somewhat similar plans. The sooner the Krauts learn what we expect of them the quicker we can get out. I'm glad to say I shall not have to see this all the way thru. For one interested in government, I find prospects of living with you a million more times more interesting.

As I predicted some time ago, fights of a personal nature are starting to break out between returned German soldiers and G.I.s who have stolen their frauleins. Most Germans seem surprised and ashamed that their young women have proven to be so easily made by the Americans. Maybe humiliated is the word for it.

I'm just about settled enough to resume my accounting work. I'm starting to wonder whether I may not have enough time to get a CPA over here.

Joe and I were discussing music, having listened to the playing of a Verdi fugue over BBC. We have come to the conclusion that whatever else their shortcomings, the British have really done a wonderful job of presenting good music.

The British have gotten "round" to starting the trials of Joseph Kapner the "Beast of Belsen" and 44 others. From here the fate of their friends seems fore-ordained. And in six weeks begin the trials at Nuremburg. I have asked for temporary duty for the period of the trial if possible—anything at all to get into the courtroom and see Frick, Hess, Goering, Streicher, and the rest. During combat I saw Franz von Papen at Dortmund. That's quite a story which I was prevented from talking about by censorship and which I shall save now until I come home.

It is pretty definite that we shall move to Darmstadt for the winter. We are hoping to move into a hotel. However cold the Heinies will be this winter the Army will keep warm enough and eat and, sadly enough, we may be the only people in Europe to have even this minimum of comfort. Every street in every town is piled high along the curbs with cut wood (there is no coal) and despite this there will be much suffering—not only in Germany about which we don't care—but among all the peoples of Europe. There will be starvation and freezing, and this war has many victims to claim before next spring. I thank God you, my darling, are not here to face the brutal weather that the civilians here will face.

I love you, sweets, keep smiling, and keep busy.

All my love with all my heart.

> Ever,
> Your, Harald

~

> September 21, 1945
> Melsungen

Lo Darling,

Today I feel better—beaucoups better. General Marshall's statement has just reached us—all two-year men and over, out, or on the way out by late winter. Since I'll be a three-year man, I feel I can hope, and offer you hope, that shortly after the first of the year I'll be on my way. The radio is playing one of our old Galveston songs, "Don't Get Around Much Anymore," and as I'm writing I feel warm all over. Of course it's still the Army and anything can happen at any time, but this is the first time I've been "included" on all this business. This is the break in the news that I've been waiting for.

Oh, darling, just think of our honeymoon next spring and never fear again of separation. The blight that covered us as well as the rest of the world is starting to lift. For our trip to Galveston I want you to have the nicest clothes you can buy.

Peace and home means to me principally you, normal living, folks, midnight snacks, my old job, our life together, the end of military living and discipline, and security.

I can't write more except to hope as I probably will in every letter that the boat will come in soon for me.

I love you, darling.
Your, Harold

〜

Hello Darling,

Day by day the discharge news gets better. Now it seems definite that I shall be on the list by sometime this winter. I find it easier to reconcile myself to a few more months knowing the end is at long last in sight. I believe we have General MacArthur's honest statement in the number of troops needed in Japan for having cracked the War Department's reticence wide open. Now we must just "sweat it out." I shall have 33 months in next Wednesday and so I imagine that I shall be among the first of the 2-year men in the ETO to come home when they get the 60 points. What it amounts to is that I'll be home as soon as they get to me in the line of discharge authorized by the Chief of Staff.

Current news here is the trial of Kramer and the other Rotters from Belsen by the British court at Luneburg. Ford Kramer and the leading defendants there can be but one verdict—death. The testimony of Mrs. Brinko, the Polish Jewess, is shocking even to those of us who thought we were hardened.

These trials will continue right thru the rest of the year, as more and more of the scum that ran Europe for five nightmarish years is brought to justice.

All this is not important, but what is important is why did the German people allow themselves to sink so far? I've been here six months and I can say that the average German is intelligent, not without courtesy and savoir faire, and not unlike the English-speaking people superficially. They don't have horns and a tail, say what you will. I believe I would find them rather nice if I allowed myself to go half-way, and the only reason I don't is that, as a Jew, I hold a deep grudge.

Then what happened to them? I think the Germans, in the tradition of Faust, sold their souls to the devil for materialism. Hitler offered them security, jobs, easy conquests, and only asked they shut their eyes to the methods he had to kill, terrorize, and rob others to give them what they wanted—without earning it. It wasn't the SS or Gestapo—it was a belief in the Nazi's ability to produce that made Germany acquiescent and blind to all the monstrosities practiced in the name of the Reich. This is a lesson we Americans must bear in mind. We had our Huey Long and have our Boss Hague who achieved power by appealing to the same motives. No matter how great a military victory we have won, let's remember that "eternal vigilance is the price of liberty." Regardless of the armchair strategists at home, Germany cannot again be a menace in our time. She is beaten and her heavy industries are being torn down. Japan is even more helpless—an insular power without a navy, air force, or the basic materials for waging war and surrounded by the great powers who will see she doesn't get them. But who's going to watch us? As we love America, let's see that we protect her in peace from the enemies within as we have so ably defended her in war. All of us who have served love America, and we know that as ex-soldiers, we must, to make our sacrifice worthwhile, be on guard as much as civilians as we have been in uniform. You don't have to wear OD to be an American, thank God.

How's the day-dreaming department, honey? Mine's working overtime, particularly these last few days. Boy oh boy—it's grand thinking about coming home to our own little place. I'd better not get started on that or you'll be reading nonsense all night.

I love you.
Ever, Harold

Melsungen, Germany
September 23, 1945

Lo Darling,

This has been a lovely Sunday on which I have done nothing con-
structive except take a walk with you—and my head was in the clouds.
I find it almost impossible to avoid living in a dream world. I simply
have to give myself a kick to remind myself I am still in Europe. The
Colonel noticed I was a little absent-minded today and asked me
whether I was deciding what color suit to buy since I know I'm not
going to be in the permanent Army of Occupation. I didn't tell him
but I was really dreaming of a cozy conversation with you.

There seems to be a lot of concern at home about the mental attitude of returning G.I.s. I can't speak for others, but I can for myself. I
don't think I've changed much. I don't expect anything from anybody
for nothing. I hope to take my place in the community, and I don't
expect to spend the rest of my life talking about the war. In fact, after the
initial overflow, I don't expect to talk about it. My appreciations have
deepened—appreciation of Mother and Dad, of my opportunities in the
store, of my possibilities in the community. Most of all, my appreciation
of you and how darned lucky we are to be so much in love.

Also, I think I recognize my shortcomings. Some are correctable,
some probably only improvable—but I have learned the value of being
myself. The biggest lesson the Army has taught me is that I am capable
of holding my own.

I'm no radical—in fact I think I'm more conservative than before.
And—oh yes—I have several more gray hairs around the temples. And
I have never felt better in my life, although I'm awfully sick of Army
chow. Paging my favorite cook!

And—I love you with a depth that would be impossible to believe
if I didn't feel it.

Your, Harold

September 24, 1945
Melsungen

Hello Sweetheart,

I'm starting to really wait for mail now, almost a week with none. What is happening is that Central Postal Directory back in Paris has stopped my mail from going to the old outfit and is rerouting it.

Yesterday afternoon a friend of mine, a sergeant in the CIC (Counter-Intelligence Corps—the Army's FBI) came over to tell me there are 15 Hungarian-Jewish girls here for a week and would I help him plan a party for them? They were slave laborers in a German munitions factory at Allendorf north of here and are being returned to Budapest. This stopover is to await transportation from here. Last night Paul Faska of Cleveland, and the *Stars and Stripes* correspondent with this division, and myself and three other guys went down to visit them. They are quartered very nicely in a house once owned by a leading Nazi of this town and now held by AMG for a refugee hostel. What happened to the Hitlerite and his family no one knows or seems to care. Most of these gals speak only Hungarian and a few speak German or Yiddish-none English. These poor girls are all sterilized—and none over 21 years old. Some are quite pretty but all show the ravages of 4 years of slavery. Their spirits are pretty high, although the few wiser ones wonder what they shall find when they get home. One, named Ilonka Schlesinger, with whom I talked mostly (she's a little older than the others and married), said she almost dreads going home because her husband may be dead—she hasn't heard from him in over a year—and she knows her parents were killed. She may have a sister left in Budapest. She kept looking at my wedding ring until I finally asked her why. Then she explained hers was taken by the Nazis when she was deported and mine reminded her of it. I felt awfully sorry for them. Incidentally, the ring was quite a protection. This is the first time I've been exposed socially to so many young girls, and all of them would like to come to America if you get what I mean.

Additionally, any Jewish-American is a prize. A couple of these girls made quite a play for the other two Jewish boys so I felt safer with Ilonka (quite a name) who is just as married as I am. It's quite tragic for them, going home to what they know-not and bearing the scars of a great indignity practiced on them by the great noble German people. Germans make me sick!

I'll bet the guys with 44 points or less are really sick—that is the real Army of Occupation. I am in the very middle of the "clean-up force" (45-59 points). Incidentally I told you I had 51 points. I don't, I have 52. That should get me home at the latest the end of March the way I figure it, and it is reasonable to come home for earlier shipment.

All my love.
Ever,
Your, Harold

September 26, 1945
Melsungen
1 P.M.

Hello Sweetheart,

I've been having a busy evening here, doing the evening shift, listening to *Information Please*—a murder mystery, finally half-completing another chapter of my accounting course, and now writing to you.

I hope your mother is feeling better now. I'm so sorry she hurt her ankle—I'll bet it gave you quite a scare! No doubt she's completely OK. Give her my love and Pappy too.

You can't imagine how much better I feel knowing the end is in sight! It doesn't seem that spring is so far away. It's just like being away to school from September until spring vacation, having somehow neglected to come home for Christmas.

Speaking of interest, we've got a kid in this battery from Creston, Ohio. He's just 19 and has 24 points and his name is Giet. His eyes fairly popped when I introduced myself. His famous first words were gulp, "I buy all my clothes at your store." He's a pretty nice little kid to have to be settling down here for a year or so. He's the first guy from Wayne County I've run into since my basic at Wallace. It felt nice to meet someone from home.

I'm glad, darling, your world revolves around me because that makes us just a pair of electrons revolving around each other. I won't rest until I can be with you, and those marvelous parents of ours. I count every day lost that I'm away and yet each is a day closer.

I'm sleepy, darling, so I'll say good night, and mentally pull the covers around you because it's cold tonight.

I love you.

Your,

Ever, Harold

∽

Melsungen

September 27, 1945

Hello Darling,

I really had a busy day today, working hard. I also got two letters from you—very, very welcome—and a nice letter from your mother.

There's a possibility I may be transferred again. All men from 50-59 points are leaving occupation forces to join the cadre of the clean-up forces in France and Belgium. I may go next week—since I have too many points for occupation and too few to go home. I imagine it will mean a transfer out of the artillery for the first time since I entered service. It will be step number one on the way home, darling, and it will mean getting out of Germany forever.

That was a very sweet letter you wrote when you told how you feel about when I'm coming. You don't know how much it means to have such swell backing. I have said it before and I will again that my state of mind depends on yours.

I've got loads of work piled up here and guess I'd better quit for now. Mainly, I want to get the hell out of this God-awful question mark of a country—once and for all. I'll never come back here again—never. I remember too much. With all my heart.

Ever,

Your, Harold

∽

September 28, 1945

Melsungen

Hello Darling,

One of the officers here just walked in and told me it was nice to have me here. That when we're all thinking of going home soon, it is a pleasure to have men who still take an interest in their work. I thanked him and said that I've always felt any job that has to be done was worth doing well. Anyhow doing it right makes the time pass faster and is no more trouble than being sloppy.

Well, it looks like I'll be staying here for awhile, so send anything to this address. The colonel will release essential men only when ordered or unless they go directly home and this was just an inter-theatre transfer, so I stay.

Joe will be back from Paris tomorrow, then I'll be able to take it easy. I've been working pretty steadily in order to give him this pass but I'm sure he'd do the same for me so I'm glad to do it. Perhaps I'll manage to get to England for Christmas.

At long last we are developing a clear-cut policy that I believe is going to become more vigorous as we go on. Isolation died with the dropping of the atomic bomb on Hiroshima. As we enter the post-war era it starts to look as we are coming of age in the State Department. On the issue of the Balkans and Poland we are going to be just as tough and realistic as the Soviets. We seem to be working out a policy—based on the traditions, aspirations, and interests of the Republic.

Not a carbon-copy of British or Chinese or Russian policy—but a series of aims of our own. We didn't win this war for Britain or anybody else but ourselves. Now I think we should implement this victory in the field by demonstrating that when we get around the green table we will ask for and bargain for the attainment of our objectives. In spite of all the lofty language and motives of the UNCIO and what will follow, each nation must be able to paddle it's own canoe to survive. We seem to have found the paddle and know where we are going in the post-war world. We are on our way to being the leader of the liberal democratic bloc in a world divided into two opposing (but not hostile) theories—democracy and communism. We can and will live in the same world peacefully with our communist fellow fighters. We shall insist on the same privileges in the world for ourselves and the weaker nations who think like us, as Russia will do for herself and her "fellow travellers." We believe there are plenty of the world's goods for all and we shall do business with and be friends of our communist neighbors, but we shall be as realistic as they in measuring the profitability of our deals. I think Jimmy Byrnes is a pretty shrewd horse trader. We are bound to be in world politics up to our necks now.

I wrote to Babbitt a few days ago—he's with the 2nd Armd. Division Artillery now, and hope to hear from him before too long.

I guess we hit the rainy season. I shall spend the evening doing another chapter in accounting and hit the hay. I still love to sleep to the sound of rain. Remember?

I'm eagerly looking forward to the arrival of your picture, darling. God, how I love you!

With all my heart—
Ever,
Your, Harold

Lo Darling,

It's Saturday afternoon and Joe just returned from Paris so I'm off for the weekend. I have nothing to do with my time but read and listen to the radio and perhaps see a movie but it's nice to be off duty for a change.

We got a liquor ration today—a bottle of Johnny Walker Scotch—but I'm off the stuff so I traded mine for 18 bars of candy and 6 packs of cigarettes.

The strike situation at home is terrific, isn't it? I read today where the garment district is closed down due to an elevator operator strike. I've no doubt it is having a paralyzing effect on the ready-to-wear business. Perhaps it will help clean out slow movers since no one else can get merchandise either.

Labor unions are again raising their heads. Two prominent anti-Nazis from Kassel have requested permission to form a "Workers Federation." Both of these men have honorable concentration camp records and were outstanding in the German Socialist party. Neither is a Jew. It is only from such people that we find a knowledge of democratic process. The very old are tired and bitter, the young are ignorant of all but Nazism. We are conducting schools among the youth. Those connected with it doubt that more than bare attention is being paid to the democratic teachings. It is such a shame because these people have everything but the soul—they just have had the instinct to do the decent thing burned out of them. The French, on the other hand, have only that left. Our course in the future is clear—between the two, Britain and the U.S. have no choice but to favor France. Funny, isn't it, that the most savage war of history should be due basically to just that.

I have one luxury here I never had at home. We have no hot water in the barracks. We have a barber for whom water is heated and every day I get a shave. Every day. Before that, it was for my wedding and one or two other times—now it's old stuff. When we move to Darmstadt in a couple of weeks, I wonder whether I will be so plebeian as to shave myself! The price set by the B.C. is 1/2 mark (5 cents).

I spoke to the 1st Sergeant today about a Christmas holiday in England. He said maybe—a typical regular Army topkick, but a pretty nice guy.

Lieutenant Aranoff asked me if I'd like to teach at the 3rd Division College until I get orders to leave. I said yes if it doesn't interfere with my shipping on schedule. He's going to let me know before recommending me. I'd like it all right but not at the expense of my shipping date. I'd do KP everyday to hold that, whenever it is.

Perhaps I'll get mail tomorrow and you'll give me some more food for thought. Meanwhile, I'll have to quit and relieve Joe for chow.

All my love, darling.

Ever,

Your, Harold

Melsungen

September 30, 1945

Lo Dearest,

This is gloomy Sunday, but I've been putting it in profitably. I had a bath, read several chapters of *Foreign Policy* by Walter Lippman, and am now listening to a concert by the Philadelphia Orchestra, Isaac Stern, violinist. He just played a Prokofiev violin concerto. He plays beautifully. I can visualize him doing it, although I've never actually seen him play. He and his anecdotes are forever a part of the saga of the Balinese Room to me.

Yesterday I heard *Traviata* from the Met with Lucia Albinese, Jan Peerce, and Lawrence Tibbetts. It was excellent. I think I mentioned that my desire for good music has increased tremendously. We won't miss any once I get home—symphonies and operas. It's one of the most completely satisfying sensations—definitely one of the better things of life. Most of the boys don't appreciate good music. Like all rare things, it is never enjoyed by many. They are now playing Stravinsky's *Firebird*.

This is the first place I've been for some time where there is no piano. Perhaps when we move to Darmstadt there'll be one.

Colonel Roberts didn't go back to the States with the 196th. He is head of a Courts Marshall Board trying some Nazis next week who ran a murder factory.

I haven't much more to say, so with all my love and all my heart.

Ever,
Your, Harold

⤸

Melsungen
October 1, 1945

Hello Honey,

Another month out of the way! I'm starting to get a little excited, though it may be 6 months early. They called for a list of MOS's from all men 50 to 59 points in order to ship replacements when our time comes to be transferred to States-bound units. I am told we should leave the 3rd Division within 60 days after which we shall be in a transfer unit. The ponderous machinery of the Army has started to work for us at long last.

I understand clothing is going to be scarce next spring. If so, tell Pop I want a suit for our vacation—in a grey tiny check if that's good style. I think my last Kuppenheimer measurements will be good. Only one thing you can be sure of—I won't wear brown or tan for a year or two! For now that's all, Liebling.

Ever,
Your, Harold

⤸

My Dearest,

Today we got word that 2/3 of the men in this Division from 45-59 points will leave for the 29th and 100th Divisions this weekend. No one knows which are included since they are picking them by MOS numbers (Army jobs). The remaining 1/3 will go within a month. The rumor factory is getting very optimistic. It's all going pretty fast now.

My accounting has dropped by the wayside these last two weeks in the combined excitement of more work, the good rumors, and now the World Series. I guess the Army isn't going to forget to bring me back (I had a round-trip ticket) after all.

We had a score pool on the first game of the Series yesterday and I won—got $10 for $1. It surely was a walk-away—when I drew my score, I didn't see how I could win. I'm lucky in love too!

We've gotten some men fresh from the States, with 10, 15, 20 points. Those guys will be here for quite a while. I really feel like a grizzled old vet now. Some of these boys finished their basic in August. To them I'm the Old Sarge. I'd will them my stripes for a tweed suit. It doesn't seem possible we have any right to dream about those things.

All my love.
Ever,
Your, Harold

Melsungen
October 5, 1945

Hello Darling,

Our present plans call for a move to Darmstadt to winter quarters.

Last evening I listened to the ball game from Detroit. Along with my great, almost consuming desire to return to normalcy, I find my interest in baseball has revived. It is important again—as one of the things in the American scene. So you can count on being a Sunday P.M. widow again a few times next summer while I eat a hot dog, drink a coke, and watch the Yanks trim the pants off our own Indians. I can almost see Bobby Feller twisting into that great windup of his! It was quite a thrill to sit here in this hick town in central Germany and hear the series, as it happened. Some of the boys posted a score by innings on the bulletin board. Just a bit of America here!

I imagine business is pretty good now. People are probably starting to think of Christmas. Even so, I doubt whether the store will beat last year's figures. When labor settles down and re-conversion is complete, we should be able to do better a year from now.

Well, the Council of Foreign Ministers has been unable to generate enough steam to keep the ball rolling. I believe the principal difficulty is that Stalin will not entrust Molotov with plenary power. I was proud of our stand—firm, courteous, conciliatory, but not appeasing. I'd rather the settlement took longer and prove to be closer to what we want. As Americans, we are testing our strength as the world's leading power. We have inherited the mantle held by Egypt, Greece, Rome, France, and Great Britain in the past. May we prove wise enough and strong enough to perpetuate a Pax Americana in our half of the world which will mean prosperity for all—and to influence a liberal Pax Russiana in Europe. We no longer need to worry about being made a tool of British policy—Britain's dependence on us is far greater than ours on her. If this be Imperialism, make the most of it, and let us hope that the influence of the Republic on the rest of the world is as beneficial as it has been for most of the citizens of our country.

Keep the cheerful letters up, honey, and every day is one closer.

All my love.

Ever,

Your, Harold

Lo Darling,

Having just heard the World Series evened up at 2 games each, I am ready for bed. It was a pretty good game but I still pick Chicago to win.

As for the low-down on Patton—he got what was coming to him. He's no more fit for occupation than Ivan the Terrible. Besides, he belongs to a reactionary Regular Army clique that serves the country well only because militarism and attendant military corps do not flourish in the U.S.

The fever over transfers seems to have cooled down a bit. I don't expect to be transferred from the 3rd now until November or December. There is a chance we will be sent home directly. But I don't expect to leave Europe in less than 4 months.

What do you think of Morgenthau's plan to leave the occupation job to the nations which suffered under the Nazi yolk? I haven't had time to really appraise it yet, but on the face of it, I disapprove. I think that as a great power we must bear our share of the work, as well as the responsibility for re-educating Germany. Mac Arthur is finally getting tough in the Pacific. I was sure he'd crack down as soon as the Jap Army was sufficiently demobilized so that the occupation forces would not be endangered. Before we're thru, they'll know who's boss—leave it to Mac.

You're quite right about this interval giving me time for some reading and study that I wouldn't have had time for were I home. I enjoy it, but may I be ungrateful enough to say that I wish I were unable to do it. In other words, home is where I want to be. I know that somewhere in some camp at home is a nice little soldier getting ready to come over here and take my place—and the sooner he gets here, the cute little 10-point man, the better.

> With all my love.
> Ever,
> Your, Harold

Melsungen, Germany
October 7, 1945

Lo Dearest,

It's eleven months today since I've seen you. Though we're far apart, what a difference. This day, as all days now, is filled with hopes and dreams and plans. The reunions that so many families are having daily will come to us too.

Some of the boys were unduly optimistic about their chances of getting home this year. I mean those with less than 60 points. True, some will, but the vast majority of us will be those sailing in the first quarter of next year. Most of us are in my boat—we are serving temporarily in the permanent occupation divisions until replacements can be sent in. Until they clear men with 60 points or more, they are not going to complicate the supply situation by bringing in still more men. It will be a matter of luck as to when I get home next year. I am trying to stay in occupation until then so that I can avoid the "clean-up" force which will be the last to go home. After January 1st, I will be eligible as soon as they send a replacement. May mine come early!

There's nothing new, just the same old rounds that keep me busy but get duller by the day. I could get transferred to more interesting MG work but fear to become essential so shall not attempt to do anything but get out—and meanwhile stay bored to death.

I'm sure your job is more interesting and I'm glad one of us is able to enjoy the days.

Hope you don't mind my dropping a tear or two on your shoulder, honey. This is a hell of a way to live, and I'm thankful that I'm probably in my last 6 months of it. I love you.

Ever and always,
Your, Harold

Lo Darling,

Yesterday I had a very interesting experience. I believe I told you about these Hungarian-Jewish refugees. I hadn't taken the gals any candy for a week or so, and we got our rations, so I went down there night before last. The C/C Sergeant who first told me about them was there and asked me if I'd like to meet a pure Aryan anti-Nazi. I said sure, so he took me to visit a local dentist, Dr. Albert, who spent a few years in a concentration camp. When Germany was running short of professional men, they released him and sent him to France with the Army. He has a lovely wife and a son of 19 who seems also to be free of the Nazi taint—oddly enough. They gave this man back his own house (from which he had been evicted in 1935 to make room for a Party man) They have a lovely home. The living room is large with books—good books—in German, French, and English lining all the walls. The furniture is modern, the taste is impeccable. I go into such detail because this is the first home lived in by civilians I have been in for seven months—since I was in England. And these people are really fine. He reminds me of Sam Freedlander—a typical intellectual. I hope to go back if we stay here long enough. Incidentally, he sees no future here for anyone. I gave him a pack of cigarettes and he was really touched. They were the first cigarettes he's had since returning here two months ago. He's been smoking tea leaves. For most Germans, they're too good but we do have to remember that there are a few good ones who fought this evil. In over 6 months here, I have found only him—the first good one. I guess it just proves that fine people are fine anywhere, regardless of nationality. He says there are many Germans who didn't like what they saw but were afraid to endanger their families or themselves by speaking out. He asked me whether I honestly thought most Americans would have risked life and limb to fight for ideals. I answered that I didn't think such a thing could go so far as to be invincible in the U.S. Incidentally, all of them fear the Russians—say they aren't "fair." Whether this is the result of Nazi propaganda that was so painful that it had an effect even on anti-Nazis, or whether there is some truth to the ugly stories of the undisciplined ravages of Russian troops in their section of Germany, I can't say. Of course I wouldn't tell them I think the Reds are entitled to a few excesses after all they've suffered at the hands of the Nazis. There are some things you can't say while a guest in someone's home—even though they hate the Nazis, they are Germans.

That's all for tonight. The World Series game is now in the 11th inning and if Detroit wins, I lose ten bucks. Oh well, the Cubs looked good a week ago.

Goodnight honey—sleep tight.

> With all my heart.
> Ever,
> Your, Harold

⌒

> Melsungen
> October 9, 1945

Lo Darling,

Today is Mom's birthday. I wrote her hoping the letter would arrive on time. Next year we'll have her birthday dinner at our house.

I didn't get on the shipment which is going to spend the next couple of months occupying Berlin. Instead Joe Atlas got it and I shall have to break in a new man. I'm going to try to do a good job because his efficiency may depend on my chances of leaving this division for one with better prospects. I spoke to the adjutant this morning on what I can expect in regard to releasing me. He said I have nothing to worry about—they like my work and will probably hold me off of inter-theatre transfers. This outfit has never held anyone who was unwilling to stay for more than a week. When they get around to asking me, I shall tell them in a clear and ringing voice that I am unwilling to stay in uniform one minute longer than I am compelled to. After I leave here, I will go to a unit alerted for shipment home. Until then, I shall be a very high point man in the division.

Joe and I have been great pals and I've spent most of the time talking with him that I should have spent studying accounting. After he goes, I should be able to get back on the ball.

Yates, who's at an outpost, was in yesterday and sends you his best. I still haven't heard from Sam Babbitt, but I imagine he's on his way home. I think it's going to be glorious to have the opportunity to re-experience the thrill of starting a life with you again. It's like being allowed to live the happiest part of your life twice.

> I love you.
> Ever,
> Your, Harold

⤳

Melsungen
October 11, 1945

Hello Darling,

The World Series is over—and I'm still waiting. The radio this morning says they are going to use 45 to 55 point men for clean-up forces. That rather contradicts the impression we gained earlier that men with somewhat longer service would be relieved after the first of the year. I don't believe that the clean-up work will last very long or involve 3-year men if it does—but what the hell? I don't even pretend to understand the War Department. I know I'll get out in the spring and any earlier return will be gravy. I'm tired of worrying about it—you can't get a clear cut answer but it keeps inching closer.

This strike "unauthorized" of Longshoremen is going to be pretty serious as regards food and supplies for us and the destitute civilians over here. That's one strike that's affecting people who shouldn't be made to suffer from any strike action. I hope the government and public opinion will crack down swiftly.

This final period before we know just when to expect the big day is very hard. During combat and even until V-J Day, I was very resigned to stay in. Now that I know the Army is going to release me, the question of how soon is important. I'm living OK, eating well, and God knows I get plenty of sleep—but I'm still restless all the time.

If the present announcement of putting men 45 to 55 points in a clean-up force goes thru, I shall probably be transferred to a unit in France or Belgium. I say if—the Army only changes plans once on the hour. Since I don't have a Chinaman's chance for an early discharge, I'll have to wait until they crawl at snail's pace to the point where I can take this damned uniform off (six more months of this). I only hope they give 3-year men a break—that would make me eligible to be discharged right after the new year. But who knows—not the lunk-heads who run the Army! I wish Congress would take the situation over. At least you'd see some Generals get canned and that would be heartening for us civilian soldiers.

Now that I've got that off my chest, I feel better. I had so hoped to be home for our anniversary and your birthday. Do you mind if we celebrate a month or two late? I'd settle for a straight 6 months more service in the States—no questions asked.

Our move to Darmstadt has been postponed. Really, I don't care. Germany is Germany no matter where you are. The only thing that will bring a light in my eyes is the sight of that statue in lower New York Harbor—that means you and home.

I love you darling, always.

Ever,
Your, Harold

〜

Dearest,

I find it more difficult to keep interested in world affairs now that I am so interested in my own status. I pick up the Stars and Stripes, look for redeployment and point news, and toss it aside.

The fellows who went to the 78th Division claim it's not a good deal after all. Moving from one division to another isn't going to do anyone any good at this stage—when they get to you—you go home wherever you are.

I've been thinking over my European adventure—it's quite a story. The trip over—Hereford, Birmingham, Cardiff, London, Rouen, the beautiful countryside of the Seine, then the two-day trip to the front via northern France and into Belgium (we slept the first night in an open field where the British suffered their first defeat in this war) and on to Liege and Namur where we spent the second night sleeping in an officers' candidate school (Belgian) and where we had our last shower for 3 weeks. Then on thru Munchen—Gladbach and Aachen, we crossed the border into Germany at exactly 4:17 P.M., March 17, 1945. I made note of that. And so, into the front before the Rhine at Lintfort where we appropriated a fine house for message center and wire section. From then on, we always lived in houses, kicking out the Krauts on a standard two-hour notice. Then we plunged into total war in the Rhineland and central Germany—occupation and the utter boredom of the police job ("which are the prisoners—we or the Krauts" used to be our watchword); the beautiful interlude in Paris— then the switch to the 196th and two months later to the 3rd. This was war! I shall not forget the towns we worked in—you don't forget those things even though they are too small to be on the map! They were, after we crossed the Rhine—Vorde, Dinslaken, Buer-Hassell,

Erkenschwick, Waltrap, Recklinghausen—from which place we moved back to Erkenschwick for a rest—kicking the same people out of their houses for the second time—did they love us? But then, we liked their modern apartments.

That was all the combat we had. From there we went to Detmold for 6 weeks—then Fulda for a month. Then the transfer to the 196th at Gersfeld just a few kilometers outside Fulda. And finally, a month ago, here. Incidentally, the pictures I sent you in which we posed with Nazi equipment were taken at Erkenschwick.

Before I close for the day, I must confess I am an awful liar. We were not 10 or 20 or 30 miles I told you from the front. We were usually about 5,000 yards from the German lines. It seems that's a relatively efficient distance from which to direct artillery fire. But that was a military secret at the time. In fact, once we got ahead of the infantry—which is how Casale got the name "spearhead" (behind his back), and that story is one that's very humorous now and you'll want to hear it in person. That's the first time in my adult life (and only one) I didn't get my pants down in time. I can look back now and laugh. We all got out OK. See how a dearth of news leads to such a rambling letter? Oh well, don't worry dear. I won't bore you with such stories after the first few days at home.

With all my love—
Ever,
Your, Harold

P.S. This letter is sort of a reminder for me—it will bring much back when we're talking together.

Lo Darling,

This is a cold and gloomy day. Particularly so for the boys waiting
in France for ships that are being held up because of strikes in
America and England. Now that the Aquitania and Queen Elizabeth
have been removed from the American run, everything is even more
cloudy. I don't see that it will affect me. I am not that close to the
gangplank yet. But I can understand the rage of thousands of G.I.s
about the strikes that are delaying their homecoming. The removal of
the two Cunards will only delay us a couple of weeks.

The latest is that we are leaving for Darmstadt in a week.

The mail isn't in yet so I'm hoping for a letter today. Meanwhile,
I'm going to take your advice—relax and stop watching the calendar. I
wish I could hibernate like a bear until spring.

> With all my heart.
> Ever,
> Your, Harold

Melsungen
October 16, 1945

Dearest,

There isn't any news today, so I thought we'd talk a little about
Britain and Palestine. I think even though we are Jews, we are not vio-
lent enough to be too one-sided.

While the Arab world expresses itself in no uncertain terms and the
President throws our great weight back of continued immigration, the
British make no decision. They seem to be caught on the horns of a
dilemma. The labor government seems, in my opinion, to be anxious
not to alienate humanitarian feelings by turning down the pleas of
Jewish remnants to return to Palestine. On the other hand, the empire
has over one million Moslem subjects who would consider it almost a

declaration of war should Britain now open up Palestine to further British entry. The Moslems in India have told Mr. Atlee what they think of the situation thru the Moslem League.

Therefore, Britain will probably stick to the closed door to further immigration. The U.S. government will un-protest but I don't think this will do any good. The guilt of leaving perhaps a million survivors of Nazi persecution will be England's. The real cause will be the system of Imperialism that forces a great civilized people like the English to choose wrong over right to save their future. The Jews of Europe might as well stop looking toward the promised land. Arab help in the war meant that no more will come in. I blame no one, but these people cannot remain in Europe. The hate campaign succeeded too well— the swastikas are gone but the effect remains from the French border to the Ukrainian frontier. God help them—these "pauvres enfants." Some refuge must be found for them somewhere. We can really thank God we are lucky to be Americans.

I'll let that be the thought for the day.

With all my love—
Ever,
Your, Harold

〜

Melsungen
October 17, 1945

Lo Darling,

I've resumed my work on my accounting course. I finally have this job down to my size.

Some of my time I spend on general reading. I'll be another month finishing *The Republic* by Beard, one of the finest books of our day. We get quite a few periodicals from which I find a lot of interest. So you see my bookworm is getting plenty of material to feed on. But even when I read, I want to do it in a den lined with books, and most important I want you there interrupting my train of thought. And finally demoralizing me so that there's nothing to do but go to the kitchen hand in hand to raid the icebox, or to head for the drive-in or Liberty for hamburgers. I guess that's why I really came over here—to make sure we could live the rest of our lives in our own way.

Here's a big hug and a kiss for tonight, darling.

All my love.
Ever,
Your, Harold

∽

Melsungen
October 19, 1945

Lo Darling,

I see where General Berry of the Adjutant General Department has said that the discharge score will have to be reduced to 50 by December 1st, if the rate is to be kept up. That still wouldn't get me home this year.

Just in case I make it in February, let's say we hit Miami before going to Galveston. That will be the southern vacation, second honeymoon, and terminal furlough all rolled into one. I warn you, I'm in a mood to do lots of reckless things just to see your eyes shine. Perhaps we'll even go to Habana for a couple of days. We're going to have long carefree days together and beautiful southern nights even if it rains.

For a long time I thought I'd be in uniform for our vacation but it looks like I'll be able to wear civvies. Yep, I now expect to be discharged before coming home. Everything's going our way.

Still expect to go to Darmstadt next Wednesday. They have a better NCO club and theatre there. Perhaps I'll get to Roosevelt Stadium (formerly Horst Wessel) in Frankfurt for a football game on Saturday afternoon. Germany now has a U.S. football league, a British rugby league, and a Russian soccer league. Everyone plays but the Krauts. On the surface, everything's OK.

All my love.
Ever,
Your, Harold

∽

Melsungen
October 20, 1945

Lo Darling;

From all they say, Darmstadt is going to be much better than here.
I have even heard rumors that we shall eat from plates and have wait-
resses—but for a year I've eaten out of a mess kit so if they don't have
such luxuries, I guess I can stand it. I know we'll have better movies
and more club facilities. I expect this to be my last stand in the ETO
and I'd like it to be as comfortable as possible since it will probably last
until the end of the year. As you've probably gathered from my letters
of the last few days, I'm getting more optimistic all the time.

I suppose you are home with Mother now. I surely hope she's feeling better and the ankle is mending well. I imagine you're kept pretty
busy and it must be fun to see the Lindheims again.

Grimaldi and Snyder shipped out to the 78th Division which is
going to Berlin—the same outfit I had wanted to go to 2 weeks ago.
Now I don't want to go anywhere but home. My letters must be getting monotonous, but I'm very lonesome for you.

One year less 18 days ago we said goodbye. But at last we're beginning to see the light.

With all my love, my darling—

> Ever,
> Your, Harold

Melsungen, Germany
October 21, 1945

Lo Darling,

We are definitely moving Wednesday morning the 24th at 8:30 A.M.
The orders came last night so there is no longer any doubt. We will be
located right in the city of Darmstadt, the first large German city in
which I shall have been stationed—and I'm sure the last. As Colonel
John said to me, we shall at least get away from the barnyard smells that

pervade these country towns I've been living in for the past three and a half months. The most important thing is that there will be a few more facilities for putting in those long evenings. For the fraternizing clan there is always plenty to do but those of us who don't have any interest in the ladies are restricted to movies, reading, and the radio. And it would be nice to go someplace where I might find a piano again.

The news about the 12 warships that are going to help bring troops home is good. I find it increasingly difficult to be calm and patient as the days drag by—toward the inevitable happy ending. I know that I must just sit tight until the first of the year.

They are now urging us to join the Reserves upon discharge. I wouldn't put on another uniform (barring war) for ten thousand dollars a day. The longer I stay here now the less anything military interests me. The Army is like a circus. Everything is always the same, which is all right if you like the life but I do not. No, I won't join the Reserves or the National Guard or anything else. I shall have put in better than a three-year enlistment when I get discharged and that is enough for me.

I wrote in this mood just to let you know that I feel mean too, now and then—so don't feel too badly when you feel the same. Also, I woke up with a headache this morning which probably accounts for it. So don't take this letter too seriously, darling—I'll feel much better tomorrow. I know you'll want to share it, and be thankful this time, at least, that I'm not there to gripe in person. Tomorrow will be another day, but if I get thru this one without punching someone in the nose I'll be lucky (because he'll probably punch back).

So on the theory that my undoubtedly cheery mood of tomorrow will stand out in contrast to my ugly one today, I shall mail this letter—

And today ... even today....

> With all my love,
> (if you'll have me)
> Ever,
> Your, Harold

Lo Darling,

Well, one day here is over and things seem to be shaping up pretty well. I have a nice office setup and my living quarters are superb—about time!

We are in an outlying section of the city—something like Cleveland Heights. We have (the first three-graders) a lovely home on a winding road something like Overlook. All the houses are nice. The trolley lines run down the side of the street in approved suburban fashion. The only difference is that some of the houses are gutted and destroyed— and next door to most of these ghosts of houses are homes untouched. In such a one we live. It's in Deutschland—the people aren't friends. The feeling I have in this wealthy suburb is more of strangeness than I had in cow towns like Gersfled and Melsungen. There the country people seemed a little less antagonistic—of course their homes and town didn't get the destruction a city like this gets. Downtown Darmstadt is a shambles—only Kassel is worse. I thought we raised hell in Dortmund and Essen and Dusseldorf, but Georgie Patton must have used some secret atomic energy during his drive thru here. Our house is located 3 blocks from the office and I counted seven destroyed homes between the two.

By the way, our house has a piano in it and I shall get back into prac-tice soon. I'm anxious to hear how it sounds—it looks like a good one.

I see you, too, fell for little Siegfried. He was cute and so far I haven't found another like him. I'm not quite as far from Gersfeld as I was before, so perhaps I'll go back and kidnap him for you.

Keep up the social activity, dear. As for me, I'm feeling much better about the whole thing now—and I'm patiently waiting again. I think I'm thru being temperamental—I'll dream of you. I'll say goodnight, darling.

With all my love—Ever,
Your, Harold

Darmstadt
October 26, 1945

Hello Sweetheart,

Today was "one of those days." Everything went wrong. One of my agents came in late last night without the stuff I sent him for. So I sent him out again this A.M. and he ran into the back of a streetcar and banged his jeep up (no one hurt). So I was short a man and with 400 miles of driving to be distributed among four agents—I fell a half-day behind in my work. I won't be caught up for a couple days.

They've got a beautiful non-coms club set up in a former road-house about 400 yards from the office. I wonder if I'll ever get time to go up there?

This morning I was down by the Red Cross Building. They have plenty of attractions—Coke bar, doughnut dugout, library, game room. I saw a couple of books I'd like to read when I can get time.

Everyone lives in a state of suspension over here. It's strange, when you stop to think of it, so many people just existing while so much time passes. While not as final, it is one of the great wastes of war.

Take good care of yourself, darling, and don't lose hope.

With all my love,
Ever, Harold

⌐

October 27, 1945
Darmstadt

Lo Darling,

Another Saturday night—loneliest day of the week—because tomorrow is Sunday and no you to be with. It's almost November and how much better it is to be on the home stretch—looking forward to 1946 with sure anticipation rather than the dread with which we faced 1945 a year ago.

Mom keeps asking what I want for my birthday, but I honestly don't want a single thing—unless I thought you could squeeze into a box and come over here—but they don't have any mail service that first class.

Now that we're in winter quarters and I am very comfortably situated, I really have less time to enjoy it because my work has almost doubled. It's just as well because I would be very unhappy if I had too much time on my hands. The work isn't much but it takes up the time. I could have gone to 3rd Division College as a history instructor but refused because it might delay my return home. I'd rather stay here in message center because I know they can replace me quickly. Incidentally, I just discovered that there is no reference on my qualification card that I can type and no one here but Yates knows it—and since typists are a critical shortage, they won't. I shall type no more letters—too big a risk because if the B.C. should catch me at it I'd be in the office pronto. I'm playing my own game now, not the Army's.

I've been very interested in the game the Soviet Union is playing in Eastern Europe, the Balkans, and her share of occupied Germany and Austria. The pattern is now clear even to one who has a great admiration for the courage and steadfastness of the Russian people such as I have.

Russia is attempting to build a bulwark of Communist-dominated satellites in Hungary, Poland, Bulgaria, and Romania. Already in Tito she has a firm ally in Yugoslavia. Even in Italy the Communist vice premier is obviously looking to Moscow over his shoulder when he makes very bold claims for what is a minority party.

I have no fear of Communism and I am no enemy of Russian internal politics. But the type of governments Russia is forcing (yes!) on these countries means that she is building a bloc of buffer states even before the guns are cool. It also means she is creating a hegemony over certain sectors of Europe which is contrary to the announced principals of Britain and ourselves as expressed in the Atlantic Charter and the reaffirmed principals of self determination (shades of Woodrow Wilson!) to which Russia herself subscribed at San Francisco. All this does not mean war, but it does mean that Great Britain and the U.S. will have to see to their own political fences in Western Europe and Latin America and that this type of maneuvering is leading slowly but surely to a Russian bloc versus an Anglo-American bloc in the void created by the disappearance of Germany as a nation. Where there is a vacuum something is bound to rush in but lots of us had naively hoped that a combined power not conflicting powers would fill it. Such is not to be.

The President and the State Department are meeting the situation as best they can—with no loss of patience but with firmness (i.e. the protest against the Soviet-Hungarian economic agreement while Hungary is still an enemy power).

G.I.s like the Russians they've met, but were close enough to see their power squeeze at short range and it doesn't look very good. Russia doesn't want war any more than we do and war between us is ridiculous. We know now Russia will need some firm handling from the democracies—she's not against us but she's not one of us either.

And so sweetheart, them's my sentiments. I have others on a more important relationship. All my love darling.

Ever,

Your, Harold

～

Darmstadt

October 28, 1945

Lo Darling,

This is a nice sunny Sunday afternoon—just the kind on which you and I would be out driving. Today I'm on duty, so it's a case of being on the inside looking out. Our work has gotten so heavy that I have divided each day into thirds—and Rollins (my assistant) and I work alternate thirds. So today I'm on in the afternoon, tomorrow it will be morning and evening, the next day the afternoon, etc. Our day begins at 7 A.M. and ends at 11 P.M.—too long for any one person day after day. This way you get some time off every day which is much better, even though you never get an entire day off. But what would we do with a whole day off?

I am just starting Carl Van Doren's *Benjamin Franklin*. I find that my interest in European history, which used to be paramount, is declining and I am far more interested in American history and all Americana in general. There is no doubt that this change is due to my participation in the war. Whereas a short 30 years ago we still looked to Europe, especially England and France, for guidance culturally and politically, we have now come of age. Twice in that period we have rescued Western civilization from the pit. In doing so we have become not the follower but the leader of the highest civilization of our day. We can still learn from Europe, of course, but we are the young, vigorous leader of thought today and the hope of the world. So to be a good citizen, we must study our own past and shortcomings and plan accordingly, because if we fail this time, God help the next generation.

With all my heart,

Ever,

Your, Harold

◡ר

Darmstadt

October 29, 1945

Lo Darling,

I went downtown by strassenbahn (street car to you) and walked around town. It is really torn up—not a whole building anywhere near the center of town. The street car was crowded coming home and I got up and gave my seat to an old lady which caused quite a few people to stare—I guess they weren't used to seeing that. These people got on the car with their bundles and talked about food shortages. (I understand enough now to know what they're talking about). They might be from Cleveland or Boston or anywhere. They look so average—these people. As I rode along with them I couldn't help but think—are these the people who have caused five wars of aggression in the last 80 years? Is that possible? Except for the shattered city going by outside and their language—they could be from Wooster. Their clothing is a little shabby but they have pride in themselves. But they are Germans. They did provoke five wars—it's in the record. Why? It isn't a racial characteristic—I'm now convinced. Has history played a horrible joke on us in creating a normal, likable people and not making it economically possible for them to survive without aggression? No—that can't be either. France and Italy have even less to go on, and neither of them has been the primary aggressor. Is it the Junkers? I don't know. I'm a little confused. But I do know this, that no people is diseased with the virus of war from birth. That propaganda is just that—propaganda. Something is wrong here with this normal appearing people. It's the damnedest thing finding them so normal and civilized on the surface. Maybe I've always been too much a believer in blacks and whites—the devil and the angels. This I know—war is hell for the little people of all countries—the people who don't start wars and who do all the dying. The big people, the tycoons, always seem to make a good thing of it. I am very thankful that I have taken my chances as an average soldier, with no pull and no favors, because now I have a perspective. It is an experience I shall always cherish, even while I regret the whole business.

That's all for tonight, honey.

Ever—with my love—
Your, Harold

Darmstadt
November 1, 1945

My Darling,

I got quite a kick out of your remark about being jealous of Ilonka—and I was proud too. I want you to be jealous, darling. If you weren't you wouldn't be in love. As for Ilonka, I wrote all there was to write. From me she got a couple packs of cigarettes, some candy, and a promise that I would try to contact her relatives for her when I get home. I guess I didn't mention it but those girls were returned to Hungary a couple of weeks before I left Melsungen. The only person you should be jealous of is little Siegfried—I really lost my heart to him.

Walt Winter turned up again—he's in the 39th FA which is here in Darmstadt. He came over last night and we had a good old bull session—Yates, Walt, and myself. Two more buddies of mine, Phillips and Williams, are up in Budingen north of Bad Neuheim and I shall try to get up there if I can. And Pietrusewicz is near, too, at Morfelden about 20 kilometers north of here but I haven't yet seen him either. Grimaldi and Snyder are in Berlin.

I may be closing up shop here, but I'm going to come back to you and that is why I can be patient. As the Hangman's Gazette says—time brings all things—and before we know it, time will bring the separation center, the trip home, and the sweetest day of my life—when I can hold you close and know that no "committee of my friends and neighbors" can ever separate us again.

With all my love, dearest—

Ever,
Your, Harold

Lo Sweetheart,

One year ago today we left Hattiesburg. The nicest thing about Hattiesburg was that it was so terrible we were glad to leave it even though the result was separation.

Some damned fool called parting sweet sorrow. There's nothing sweet about it.

I've really been in the Army a long time. In less than two months I shall be wearing a hash mark—3 years service. I can't say the first 22 months were tough, but the last 12 have not been so hot. All the difference has been you—when I had you with me it all seemed like a lark—but the minute you were gone it became pretty dull. I really treasure those 22 extra months together.

Even though I may not actually be with you for several months yet I feel that it's all over but the snail's race down the home stretch. Soon we can have our own little home again, and I'm living for that day.

With all my heart, darling—

I'm yours, Harold

〜

November 4, 1945
Darmstadt

My Darling,

I was pretty busy all day and in the evening I was invited to a party for the first sergeant who is going home for 90 days.

This party was lousy—with a capital "L." I don't believe in prohibition but there should be a course in school on how to hold your liquor. Too many people (and I'm afraid this applies to overseas G.I.s rather generally) drink—no, swill—liquor ad nauseam—literally and figuratively. They must enjoy it because some of them get drunk every night. That group is a minority, but you'd be surprised how many get drunk frequently. I make no claims to any special moral attributes but I thank God I have really no taste for the stuff and have a sensitive stomach to boot—I just don't care much for it so drink in moderation. Not so, most of my "worthy colleagues" among the NCOs. Some of them drink a hell of a lot and show it. Which leads me to observe that if a man wants to make a fool of himself no one can stop him. Oh well, a few more months and I won't be associating with such people. If I have to be with drunks it would be nice to be with some who had some brains. Fortunately there are a few nice fellows around.

A pile of work just came in so I'd better quit now and dig in. All my love, darling, and a great big kiss.

> G'night—dear,
> Ever,
> Your, Harold

෧

Darmstadt
November 5, 1945

Lo Darling,

This is a cold, grey day—typical weather for November. Just think, in a week I'll be 32 years old. Though it will be hell to have to spend another birthday away from home, I know this will be the last of three spent that way.

So far only one package you sent has come and everything in it was eaten long ago. I hope more come soon because I get terribly hungry at night. The food is OK but not very appetizing and very often I can't eat a whole meal anymore—just push it away. After so much Army cooking you get completely fed up with the mass preparation of food. Also I think I'm a little nervous most of the time—at least my stomach is, and so I purposely don't overeat. I find I have to keep a very tight rein on my emotions now or I'm liable to blow my top at anyone who happens to be in the way. It's a natural reaction to the strain you're under when you hate where you are and what you're doing. It will be gone the moment I know when I can expect to come home. And it's nothing to worry

233

about—just a state of mind at this moment. Some people take it out in getting drunk or in other ways. I hope you don't mind my talking to you about my moods—it makes me feel much better when I share with you—even unpleasant things. In fact, I feel better already.

I have a real League of Nations here among my agents. One is a full-blooded Indian, one a Japanese-American, one a West Virginia hill-billy, one from the sidewalks of New York, and the other a farm boy from East Palestine, Ohio. My code clerk is from Fresno, California, so you see we cover the country.

I dreamed about us last night. It was a lovely dream—very private. Perhaps that is why I'm a little out of sorts today. To be with you in dreams and to wake up so far away is terrible. But we must look forward.

With all my love, darling,

Your, Harold

≈

Darmstadt
November 7, 1945

Lo Darling,

My thoughts today are a conglomeration. I can't seem to sort them out properly. But thru the poignant memories of everything we've had together in the years before runs a strong and confident hope. It's built on the knowledge that we've withstood a whole year of this.

I will confess I'm not a bit more used to being without you than I was an hour after you left and I sat in the USO writing the first of what has become a flood of letters. They'll stop coming when I don't need paper and pen to be with you.

I think we can congratulate ourselves that we've ridden the longest and worst part of this. So, a bouquet to you, my darling—for being lonely, loyal, and a more sensible girl than I could ever deserve. We've chalked off 12 lousy months now, and we'll breeze thru the rest.

I'll be loving you—always,
Harold

≈

Lo Dearest,

We haven't had any snow yet but today is cold and raw and rainy. The climate here is much like home this time of year.

It appears the peace in China is going to be of tragically short duration. The lack of fundamental unity which has plagued the young Chinese Republic since the Revolution of 1912 which overthrew the Manchus is again causing trouble. I am afraid there is dirty work at the well-worn crossroads. I should not be surprised to learn that Russia is backing the Communist government and we and the British are behind the Generalissimo. It will all be taken out on the poor Chinese people—the rest of us won't fight but we'll jockey for position. All this is conjecture. It's a terrible pity, but I imagine we'll be completely over this experience and keep reading every day in the Plain Dealer about new outbreaks in China. I've seen enough war to be sorry for anyone anywhere who must go thru it.

Being in the Army has plenty of disadvantages, one of the most serious of which is the utter lack of privacy. Ever since I took you home a year ago I was living too close to a crowd of people. I am pretty gregarious but after a while that becomes a grievance. You long for a little retreat—a place you can go to write, read, sleep—without having a hundred people barging in and out all the time. This feeling has grown especially since hostilities have ceased. In my present setup, is the first time I have been able to have a room of my own—nicely furnished with a comfortable bed. If I want to read late, I can—and if I want to sleep early all I have to do is turn out the lights. It's marvelous and is the first advantage I've ever found in being a Staff. On the dressing table next to my bed is the folder with your pictures in it—it's the last thing I see at night and the first in the morning. The old biddy who makes our beds and cleans up said the other day—"*Ist das dein Frau?*" I said, "*Ja,*" and she said, "*Sie ist prima*"—which in English

235

means—you're the tops. So you meet with German approval, too, mein Frau.

Some months ago I was taking German lessons but I didn't stay interested long because I had no need to speak German. I still need it very little but I sometimes use it when talking to the hired help. We employ 49 Germans in menial capacities. After being here for seven months I find I can express myself pretty well in simple German. I believe I could learn to speak it quite well were I to make a halfway attempt.

Speaking of our German help, all our kitchen police work is pulled by Krauts, and now that we have dishes again, it takes about five of them. They clean the offices, officers' and sergeants' quarters—make the beds, shovel the coal, wash the vehicles, shop service, carpenter shop, paint shop. They get paid out of funds raised by taxes or levies from the populace by the burgermeister—not a cent of their pay is charged to the American taxpayer, except for certain specialists such as trusted interpreters. These trusted specialists are paid by the U.S. government Their help is invaluable to us.

Lots of civilians are continually making a nuisance of themselves by reporting neighbors for petty and even serious alleged violations of military regulations. These are grudge affairs usually but they have to be run down. A people in defeat is not a pretty sight.

We have just had a teletype machine installed here in Message Center. I am learning to run it for emergencies when the operator isn't here. It's a wonderful machine—sends a typewritten message into another typewriter 150 miles away in 1/100 of a second—and receives too. If I had reason to I could reach the Pentagon direct in 5 minutes.

Well, darling, I have once more run out of talk.

Forever Your, Harold

Lo Darling,

The Palestine controversy has become a very serious business. The riots in Cairo and Tripoli, as well as the high-handed utterances from King Ibn Saud of Arabia, show only too well how successful the Axis was in stamping its vicious breed of discontent on the Near East. The extreme Zionists haven't helped their cause a bit by their lawless disregard for the law of the land. Illegal immigration at this time should be supported by all Jews who have seen how hopeless central Europe is going to be for the survivors. I don't believe that anyone, least of all the Jewish population, is going to benefit from revolt against the British, who are in a ticklish spot. If this keeps up, the Jews of Palestine will lose all the gains they have made in the past 27 years. Whether we are Zionists or not we can't help but support it temporarily until the storm dies down.

Keep well and healthy.

Always—my love, sweet—

Ever,

Your, Harold

Darmstadt
November 10, 1945

Lo Darling,

This afternoon I did something which for me is very unusual—I took a nap. I was off duty and it was raining so I went down to the house, "tickled the ivories" for half an hour, took a hot bath, and lay down. No one woke me and I had to hurry to eat and get here by 5:30. I feel fine and rested.

You'd be surprised how many fellows are reenlisting—mostly because they've fallen in love with German girls with whom they are living and whom they want to marry.

I was just interrupted for 15 minutes—Willy and Phil phoned to talk for 10 minutes long distance on the government's time, then one of the cooks came in with a Leica and took a couple of time exposure shots of me at my desk.

The kids call me rather frequently and it's like a voice from home to hear them say, "Harold—this is Phil," or "this is Willie." Walt Winter is in town here and I see him now and then. Just waiting till they say I can hurry home to you.

All my love, sweetheart—

And, please dream of me—

Ever,

Your, Harold

Darmstadt (of all places on)

November 12, 1945

Hello Sweetheart,

Thanks for your birthday wishes. Although I have now reached the ripe (old or young?) age of 32, I have never felt younger or more vigorous.

Birthdays make you retrospective and I've thought over lots of years today. I remember when I was just a little fellow and how exciting Mother made them for me. And as I grew up we had parties—what a big crowd we had sometimes—I remember 17 at the table once. We always had ice-box cake. That's one little item Mom is going to have to make when I get home—just a warning, Mom. I remember all the birthdays since—the one in 1937 when you were going to come from Cleveland but couldn't because some wretch took you to a game at State. Then in '38 when we were engaged and you were there—and the ones since—all we had at home and the one in Galveston. I know this is the last one away from you and the folks.

No one here knows it is my birthday and I deliberately have left it that way.

On occasions like this I always stop and think how lucky I've been. I've been blessed with wonderful parents who have always done everything for me that could be done. I only hope that I now can reciprocate. And, while you've "heard that song before," I must repeat that I've got the only girl I've ever known that I want for a wife—the only girl whose very presence has always given me a unique thrill. Even being over here, bad as it is, has some little measure of compensation. I know it isn't for long. I know I at least served my country in a crisis, and I know that as a person I have been immensely benefited by being one of the crowd. It has given me a measure of confidence I didn't have 3 years ago. I still have to prove myself, but now I know I can do it. The Army, God bless it with all its faults, is not only a great leveller—it has a way of teaching you what you really are made of—in battle and out.

I love you, darling,

> Ever—
> The Old Man
> (but still young enough)

        ↩

> Darmstadt
> November 13, 1945

Hello Darling,

One disadvantage of this business of a few fellows living in a private house is that you sometimes have to make the fire yourself. That's what happened tonight. I came home and found the fire out and so I had to go down, start one, and get it going. It was the first furnace fire I'd ever built but when you must do something, you can. However, I do not like to shovel coal and so I think we'll be better off with gas, even though you can now add to my qualifications that I can keep you warm in a coal-heated home.

Today was one of the busiest I've had for some time and I actually didn't get to do a bit of my accounting work. Tomorrow I'm on duty.

Since it now seems certain I'll be over here until after the first of the year I'd very much like a leave to England for Christmas. We are only a little over half strength now, and until the replacements from the States get here there isn't much chance of any head of a section getting to go away. I'd like to go, because while I have very little actual work I have had only one day off duty in the last two months, Sundays included. But I won't mind too much—the vacation I really want will be with you.

I'm pretty tired this evening. I worked until after 12 last night.

All my love, darling, and keep planning for that big vacation this spring—

Always—
Your, Harold

↬

Darmstadt
November 14, 1945

Lo Darling,

I have put in application for a 3 weeks' course in Retail Management in England from November 26 to December 15, and there seems to be a good chance I'll get to go.

2 hours later—1 P.M.

It happened! I've been approved and selected for the retail management course. By the time you get this letter I'll be on my way to merry old England. The course is an on-the-job training course in British department stores. I imagine I'll return to Darmstadt about Christmas. I'm so damned excited—next to coming home this is the best thing that could happen. It will be a change, a chance to improve myself, and a sort of reintroduction to my business. My fingers will be crossed until I board the train at Frankfurt.

Just think—back to England. I'll write you but you can't write me there. There'll always be an England—

All my love, Ever—
Your, Harold

↬

Lo Darling,

I got two cartons of cigarettes from your folks today, plus a tin of those Round-the-World cookies from you, a birthday card, a letter from Mom, and one from you—the first good "mail call" I've had in two weeks. Thanks awfully.

We just got orders today to ship all 60 pointers and over by the 20th, so since that will leave the battery very short I'm hoping and praying the B.C. doesn't decide to get my travel orders canceled. That would be a blow especially since I've gotten all excited. If he doesn't do anything the next 30 days it will be too late, and those who know him say he'll let it go thru. I'm really looking forward to this. I surely hope that by the time I get back it will be my time to start home.

All my love—as always.

Ardently—
Your, Harold

Darmstadt
November 16, 1945

Lo Darling,

Tonight is the night I sweat it out. I'm waiting for my official travel orders for England to come thru. They are due either tonight or tomorrow night. I found out today what city I'm going to. It is Bristol, the huge west coast port across the Bristol Channel from Cardiff where I spent such a pleasant few days last January. Also it is a 2-hour drive from Hereford and perhaps some Sunday I shall go back for a few hours just to see what it looks like now that the war is over. Yes, I'm very excited about going. I don't think the B.C. will cancel my orders, now that he has approved them.

It certainly is a good thing I sent for my low-cut shoes. I would have felt funny going to Bristol to a department store in combat boots! Between the folks and everyone I have now almost 4 cartons of cigarettes. I'll need them in England, too, because I doubt whether I'll be able to get PX rations. We may still have a Navy Depot at Bristol.

Since I'll be there for some time I'm going to try to get something for all of you. I may not get up to London more than once or twice, but I'm close to Bath (the exclusive spa) at Bristol and I shall certainly do some heavy Christmas shopping.

All my love, darling—and all my kisses too—for always.

Your, Harold

〜

Darmstadt
November 17, 1945

My Darling,

Today was a terribly busy day. I had to get my orders, my train reservation, have my clothing checked, and have my money approved which was not finished until 6 this evening. I'm all set to go—a bath and a good night's sleep after I finish packing and I'll be off to Britain. On top of everything else we had a busy day in the Message Center.

All my best to the folks.

All my love to you, darling—

Ever,
Your, Harold

〜

Lo Darling,

I have a 12-hour layover here and am doing a little Christmas shopping. In addition to that I had time to take a long walk up the Boulevard Hausmann to the Montmartre and have a drink at the Café de la Paix.

I enjoyed my stroll thru the Parisian boulevards. Paris is easily the most beautiful city in the world. It's like a gorgeous woman—dangerous, expensive, and compelling.

I had cognac at the Café de la Paix and watched the pretty Parisiennes go by—I always look, as I think I once told you that when a man stops looking he's dead.

I'm going to Camp Home Run to get a boat across the Channel. That camp is still run by the 219th, so I expect to renew some old acquaintances tomorrow and get good boat service.

I've got to get my reservation at the Gare St. Lazare yet, so I'll have to run. All my love, sweetheart, and though this is the City of Light— it's a hollow light without your eyes to look into. I shall really enjoy Paris when I can bring you here.

> A million kisses—
> Ever,
> Your, Harold

∽

Camp Pall Mall, France
November 20, 1945

Lo Darling,

This camp, named like all the tent city camps, after a cigarette, is large. It has a capacity of about 2,500 troops. During combat it, along with Lucky Strike, Chesterfield, Old Gold, Twenty Grand, Home Run, was used as a replacement depot (called by all GIs "repple depples") for troops arriving from the States to get everything in order before going up to the front. The larger ones are processing troops for home while the small ones like this one take care of leave and school troops for the U.K. composed entirely of tents. The day room is OK. They have a nice shower, and I went to a barber for a shave.

The village has a picturesque beach with huge boulders jutting into the water, and towering limestone escarpments flanking it both north and south. That's good for a 10-minute look.

We shall probably spend most of tomorrow sleeping and taking it easy and waiting for that boat. This is not any luxury place, but I can stand it especially since I remember being at Twenty Grand in March on my way to combat instead of to a Bristol department store.

Last night I took care of my ticket and then went to the casual mess at the Gare d'l'Est for chow. On the way back I saw a huge crowd of Communists denouncing de Gaulle. There were gendarmes all over the place so I decided it was no place for a foreigner and took off down the Rue de la Paix. I saw swarms of people all over the section and cut back to the Boulevard Haussman and stopped at the New York Times building to see what was up. Of course I knew—de Gaulle had called for a showdown—but I didn't honestly believe Paris would have another of her famous riots. At the *Times* they wouldn't say much so I strolled on down the street. At St. Lazare there was a deGaullist crowd getting set to march to the Opera. What happened when they met the Communists up there I don't know because I had to get ready for the train. But that's one of the millions of political disturbances so much a part of Paris that I saw developing with my own eyes. If the two forces met, I'll bet there was bloodshed. There's plenty of tension in the air there.

Au 'voir—and I love you.

Ever,
Your, Harold

⌐

Lo Darling,

I can't put in words the feeling I had Thursday when the *Marchal Joffre*, the French steamer, docked at Southampton. It was almost like a homecoming for me, even though I don't know a soul in the U.K. It's just a sense of security and friendliness which is impossible to describe. Just as 11 months ago, I feel very much at home here. Last evening I made the rounds of a few pubs and enjoyed talking to some Britishers at the bar. I got into quite a discussion of the atom bomb with a couple of Tommies.

This afternoon at 3:15 I leave for Bournemouth, the Miami Beach of English resort towns, to spend three weeks at the best department store there, named Bobby & Co. Ltd. I shall cable you from the Red Cross.

All my love, sweetheart, and all my best to the Folks.

Ever,

Your, Harold

⌣

Bournemouth
November 25, 1945

Lo Darling,

I am finally at my destination—arrived here at 9 last evening.

This is a beautiful spot. I had intended to get private quarters, but I can't resist the Red Cross here. This is known as the most beautiful Red Cross Club in the world and it certainly is swanky. It is in the Carlton Hotel, which is one of the resort hotels of this "Miami" of England. The hotel is located on a cliff overlooking the ocean and the miles of beach stretch out in front of the broad lawns. The food is excellent (they have a snack bar open until 2:30 in the morning), there are three or four beautiful lounges, and a lobby that reminds me of the Essex House. This is the real G.I. luxury spot of England.

I haven't been into town yet but they say it is the most modern city in England. I have until noon tomorrow to report at the store I'm going to be with. I shall do a little exploring this afternoon.

This hotel is much like the Galvez. It's not crowded. There aren't too many troops in England any more, and it only fills up on Saturday evenings—just like Galveston! In fact the resort atmosphere reminds me of it and I miss you very very much in such a setting.

Tonight I'm going to a Pops Concert at the Pavilion. I bought a ticket for the Mikado. There is lots of entertainment here including legit theatre straight from Leicester Square. So I am looking forward to a very enjoyable three weeks—the first civilized three weeks I shall have spent in over a year.

I miss you, darling, and when I look out the window of my room at the sea, I am very lonely because it would be so perfect if your head was on my shoulder and I could steal a kiss.

I love you.
Ever, Harold

Southampton
November 30, 1945

Lo Darling,

These last four days have been a nightmare for me. About an hour before your cable came I was informed I had an emergency furlough. Then your cable at Bournemouth confirming it. I had no idea until this afternoon when Dad's cable came what I was getting it for, and I still am terribly anxious because I don't know how ill Mother is.

You can imagine my feelings as I rushed from Bournemouth to Bristol for my records, then from Bristol to London for orders, then down here two days ago for shipping orders, etc. Now I've done all I can, am alerted for shipment, and must try to be patient until I can get home. Everyone's been marvelous—if only I hadn't lost the four days it took for this stuff to get to me from Darmstadt.

I pray, God, Mom is going to be OK, and I know she's getting the best of everything. Tell her I am thinking of her constantly and am hurrying to her as fast as I can.

I have looked forward to my homecoming for so long, and now I don't know how to feel under the circumstances. I can only hope that she will be much better and that we can all have the happy Christmas we all deserve together.

This will probably be my last letter until I see you, darling.

Hoping and praying for the best—

Ever your adoring, Harold

꿍

Southampton
December 3, 1945

Dear Lo and Folks,

Our sailing has been put off until Wednesday. That will make it one week exactly from the time my orders were cut until I actually sail.

I guess this one day setback isn't so serious. But I hope it will be the last one and within a couple of days I shall be on my way to you.

I'll say goodbye from Europe today—and proceed to bite my fingernails.

All my love, Harold

꿍

Indiantown Gap, PA
January 6, 1946

Lo Darling,

I arrived at the Gap at 8 this morning. We got into Harrisburg at 5 and I ate breakfast there before coming out here. By noon I was on orders to be discharged and since that time I've had my clothing checked and have turned in all my G.I. equipment and clothing except that which I'm entitled to take home. Tomorrow the processing continues and I hope to be home Friday at the latest.

It's good to know I'm actually on discharge orders and that this is the last mile of my military career.

I really can't think of anything else to tell you, lover, except that I miss you so much, but it's almost a joy because we will be reunited in such a few days.

Love to all, Harold

~

From a Speech Given at Wayne College Fifty Years Later

We were at the Nazi concentration camp at Bergen-Belsen, south of Hamburg, in Western Germany. We, the 219th Field Artillery, arrived there on April 20th and relieved a British Infantry unit who had liberated the camp. There were twenty-two S.S. Guards who had been imprisoned when the camp was taken over by the British. Where the rest of the Germans were—we never knew. So far as we knew, we had several hundred ex-prisoners to be taken care of, and be returned to their homes.

Most were in terrible shape—they were all victims of severe malnutrition and many were ill. Nearly all were Western European Jews from France, the Netherlands, Belgium, and Germany.

Stacked up like cordwood, stored in wooden crates in large sheds, were thousands of corpses—in one must have been Anne Frank. Some of them were alive when the British arrived, but too weak and sick to be saved. The death rate during the couple of weeks we were there was thirty to forty per day. We, like the British, did our best to help them, but for many, it was too late. We never knew, or were able to ascertain much detailed information about the people we—quote-unquote— liberated, but our best estimates were that the majority were French Jews. In this camp, there were no gypsies although plenty were liquidated in concentration camps in Western Germany.

Since we were assigned there for only about two-and-a-half weeks, we were only able to start repatriating these people—by feeding them, securing medical aid and trying to find out information so that we and our successors (the French Army) could try to get them to their homes in Germany, France, Belgium, and the Netherlands.

It was our hope that many of the survivors made it but since we were succeeded at camp by French infantry, we never knew how many of these people made it home alive.

We did our best to save all those we liberated. I'm sure we did save some, and our successors saved even more because by the time we left, the war was nearly over and the healing and saving process was able to be pursued more vigorously.

A day or two before V-E Day, Adolph Hitler committed suicide, in Berlin—probably the only positive thing he did in his life.

I hope the citizens of Western Europe never again have to face the horrors of the Third Reich.